O C E A N

MILES

0   50   100   200

RANGE

S K A

•Fairbanks

C A N A D A

RANGE

TALKEETNA
MTS.

WRANGELL MTS.

Anchorage

CHUGACH

MTS.

ST. ELIAS MTS.

KENAI
PENINSULA

COOK INLET

Prince
William Sound

Juneau

Sitka

Ketchikan

Aleutian Islands

52°

AMCHITKA
ISLAND

176°   180°   176°

152°   148°   144°   140°   136°   132°

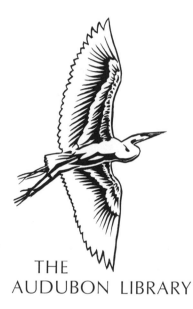

THE
AUDUBON LIBRARY

ALASKA

The Embattled Frontier

ALASKA

1971 : PUBLISHED IN COOPERATION WITH THE NATIONAL

by George Laycock

With an Introduction by Les Line

*illustrated with photographs
and maps*

The Embattled Frontier

AUDUBON SOCIETY BY HOUGHTON MIFFLIN COMPANY, BOSTON

Much of this material appeared
in somewhat different form in *Audubon* magazine.

Frontispiece: The Wrangell Range in southeast Alaska.
U.S. Geological Survey Photo by Austin Post

The endpaper and the map on page 177
are drawn by Graf-Tech.

First printing   w

International Standard Book Number: 0-395-12345-3
Library of Congress Catalog Card Number: 79-120826

Printed in the United States of America

Introduction

WITH GEORGE LAYCOCK'S informative and eminently readable introduction to America's last frontier — its land, its wildlife, and its
now familiar crisis — the National Audubon Society and Houghton
Mifflin Company launch a new publishing venture. We call it The
Audubon Library. This first volume, like some of those to follow,
is an expansion of a series of articles which originally appeared in
the pages of the society's bimonthly magazine, *Audubon*. Others
will be original manuscripts by members of *Audubon*'s respected
team of contributing authors. Their subjects may be conservation.
Or the intricacies, the wonders, the joys of the unspoiled world.
The future of this planet may often seem grim. Yet there is much
left to enjoy — and wage battle for.

This first title is not expected to be a best seller in Alaska. And
before an outraged editor of a newspaper in our forty-ninth state
shouts it in headlines, let us freely admit that George Laycock is a
carpetbagger, an outsider writing about a place 2600 miles from his
home in Ohio. He is what the *Nome Nugget* labels, in its more polite
moments, an "Eastern obstructionist." He merits this epithet because he believes that the resources and treasures of Alaska belong

to everyone in this country — in and out of Alaska. And that's an unpopular view up north.

To quote the editor in Nome further: "The obstructionists are emotionalists. They don't want us to have a pipeline; they want us to be overrun by wolves; they don't want us to have oil; they don't want us to have a highway to the Arctic; they don't want us to develop our resources. They simply sit on their fat butts back in N'Yawk and criticize us. To hell with them! Alaska was built by Alaskans, not by a bunch of lunchtime martini drinkers; but by a hardy, proud lot of people."

Such sentiments are heard again and again. And from people who should know better. Alaska's senior United States Senator, Theodore F. Stevens of Anchorage, reviled distinguished scientists invited to a University of Alaska conference, saying: "I'm fed up to here with people who try to tell us how to develop our country . . . who come up here and try to tell us what to do." He called environmental safeguards for the proposed trans-Alaska oil pipeline "stupid, absolutely stupid." And after defining ecology as the relationship between living organisms, he declared that "there are no living organisms on the North Slope."

And then there was the letter to a concerned citizen in the "Lower 48" from the chairman of the Resources Committee of the Alaska State Legislature, Joe McGill of Dillingham: "May I assure you Alaska is capable of handling its own resources. At present we have regulations and competent people to see that the wolf does not become extinct . . . If you are truly interested in the preservation of the wolf, feel free to transplant as many of Alaska's wolves as you wish in New York."

Alaska was indeed built by a hardy, proud lot of people. And one can understand resentment over what many, if not most, Alaskans regard as meddling in frontier affairs. But a lot of this resentment is inflamed by intemperate prose in local newspapers. When an economic bonanza is jeopardized, it is hard to be objective. So perhaps the best response to all this would be to answer a question, rhetorical though it may have been, posed by the *Nome Nugget:* "Whyinhell don't you mind your own business?" Quite clearly, we are. Alaskans have no more right to recklessly destroy their state's wildlife and wild beauty than Californians have the right to destroy Yosemite, or Floridians the right to destroy the Everglades. Their natural treasures belong to the nation.

George Laycock's credentials to write this book are beyond question. No conservation writer in America is more respected by his peers. He has been honored with the coveted Jade of Chiefs ring of the Outdoor Writers Association of America. As a field editor for *Audubon,* he has tackled the toughest assignments offered — the alligator poachers, the pesticide peddlers, the mountain strippers, to name only a few. He has made numerous trips to the far north, including two extended visits to Alaska for *Audubon.* He traveled to the far reaches of the Aleutian Islands to see the destruction of Amchitka Island. He followed the oil-pipeline route to Prudhoe Bay to witness the wreckage already left by the oil exploiters.

And not one of the major problems of The Embattled Frontier has been resolved since his visits. Still more underground nuclear blasts are scheduled for the sea otters' home at Amchitka, an outrageous assault on a national wildlife refuge. Not a single wilderness area has been set aside in the magnificent forests of southeastern Alaska; the lumber, every board foot of it, is destined for Japan. The great game populations of Alaska are being decimated at an accelerating rate by illegal hunting as unscrupulous guides cater to the quick-trophy trips of visiting "sportsmen" from down below.

As for Alaska's oil, there are a lot of questions to be answered before this liquid wealth is tapped. Will it be shipped out by pipeline to Valdez, by a pipeline through Canada, or by supertankers crashing through the Arctic ice? Does America really need the Alaska oil immediately for "national security" reasons, or do the oil companies actually intend to sell most of it to Japan? Can't we wait until technology offers a truly safe way to remove the oil, without risk to the ecology of the fragile North Country?

It is obvious, as George Laycock makes clear, that Americans everywhere have cause for concern over what is happening to Alaska. Those Americans include Alaskans.

Les Line
Editor, *Audubon*

Contents

ALASKA

The Embattled Frontier

Trappers Lake in the Susitna Valley, one of Alaska's most important migratory waterfowl areas. *Alaska Pictorial Service*

1

Alaska's Land and People

FROM THE FORESTED SLOPES above Ketchikan to the edge of the Arctic Ocean and the tip of the Aleutians, Alaska remains a wilderness world. In her vast marshes life begins for the wild geese; across the open tundra the restless caribou wander; and in the deep forests of the southeast live black bears, deer, and trumpeter swans. Grizzly bears, the world's largest moose, and the most magnificent salmon continue to be found here. And her people, few in number for so large a land, live near the untrammeled wild places and breathe air still largely free of chemical hazards.

Alaskans, even more than outsiders, are impressed with the sheer size of their state. Here is a single state whose borders embrace 586,400 square miles, more land than claimed by California, Oregon, Washington, Nevada, and Arizona combined. Alaska's shores stretch in a great arch for 3200 miles extending through four time zones. A single borough, the Matanuska-Susitna, famed for 70-pound cabbages and Mount McKinley, is about the size of Texas.

But not until you have traveled about this far northern state do you begin to sense what distance alone means to her people. You begin to understand, as you travel nearly 2000 miles from the southeast out across the Aleutian Islands, fly over the Brooks Range in a small plane and down the Arctic Slope to the edge of the ice-bound ocean, or up the valley of the Yukon. I recall a trip into that broad marshy world where the waters of the mighty Yukon and Kuskokwim Rivers finally reach the Bering Sea.

The first leg of the journey was by a comfortable modern airliner, from Anchorage westward to Bethel. Commercial airlines connect remote little communities throughout Alaska, and this airline, started in the 1920's by pioneering fliers Noel and Sigrud Wien, today ferries passengers and supplies to more than a hundred such locations around Alaska. But beyond the commercial routes, smaller planes fan out over the countryside into valleys, islands, and mountain passes where there are no highway links with the world outside.

In Bethel I was met at the airport by Cal Lensink, a lanky professional wildlife biologist, manager of the Clarence Rhode National Wildlife Range, among the largest areas in the national wildlife refuge system. Bethel, at the mouth of the Kuskokwim River, is a town whose people have long been fishermen, taking their livelihood from the sea and rivers. The streets are unpaved and the village plain, but its isolated location holds an appeal for its citizens.

Refuge headquarters is on the edge of Bethel. But here you are still 120 miles from the refuge boundary. As soon as we could get Lensink's single-engine plane loaded, we took off from the calm waters of a nearby lake. The wisdom of mounting the plane on floats was apparent at once. Beneath us was the delta country of the Kuskokwim and then the Yukon, coming to the end of its 1800-mile course at the edge of the sea. Branches of these streams turn and twist and intermix across the imperceptible slopes. And in addition, the tundra is marked with thousands of pools of all shapes and sizes shimmering in the sun as you pass above them.

Almost at once we were beyond signs of human activity. There were no longer any highways, buildings, power lines, trash dumps, or the inevitable fifty-five-gallon oil drums man leaves to decorate the Arctic. We saw pairs of brilliantly white whistling swans resting on the little lakes, and swift-flying formations of black brant and emperor and Canada geese passing back and forth beneath us. Each time we spotted more swans, Cal, who was carrying on a longtime population study of the birds, jotted numbers onto a tablet strapped to his leg.

There would have been no way for me to have known when we crossed the border of the refuge except that Cal told me. Within the 2.8 million acres, there was only an extension of the vast, marshy delta country, certainly one of the continent's most important nesting areas for such species as the emperor goose, cackling goose, white-fronted goose, and other assorted waterfowl. This is wilderness in fact, which one hopes will become wilderness by official designation. Elsewhere, this much land would hold a multitude of man's works, but here the land and its water belong to the birds, and it seems not too big at all in view of the needs of the wild creatures and the total size of Alaska.

Increasingly, as you travel about Alaska, you discover that her citizens have a sense of respect for the wilderness. There is still evidence of how the frontier draws people together for mutual protection. One afternoon, after a day in the field, five of us returned from widely scattered refuge locations to Old Chevak and the little frame headquarters building.

Assistant refuge manager Jerry Hout switched on the radio. Everyone sat down to listen. People "outside" might have snickered at the unsophisticated program as an announcer consumed the alloted time by reading personal messages sent between friends and relatives.

"Mary Knugluk, we will be coming back on Friday. Go ahead and sell the refrigerator. Fredrick."

"To Elizabeth Mannings. Jerry wants you to know he got the job. Repeat. Jerry got the job."

"To Benjamin Kneulting. The package arrived in good condition. The children send their love. Susan."

Beyond the cities, this "Ptarmigan Telegraph" links lonely outposts of the northern wilderness together. "I received a message that way once," Jerry Hout said. "We had a medical emergency and this was the only way to get word. Everyone up here listens to the program."

Alaska's terrain renders generalizations difficult and sometimes hazardous, but its dominant geographical features can be separated into four major areas. Along the state's northern border lies the Arctic Slope. Technically this North Slope reaches from the ocean's tidewater lagoons to the divide in the Brooks Range, but it is more commonly considered to be the rolling foothills and the coastal plains.

The Brooks Range is dominant enough on the Alaskan landscape to justify considering it alone as a feature of the state. This broad band of mountains is the northern extension of the Rocky Mountain range, and in Alaska it swings westward across the state. At its highest elevation the Brooks Range rises to 9239 feet at the peak of Mt. Michelson 65 miles from the Canadian border. It is a field of broken, sharp-edged mountains with narrow valleys. There are few lakes, but several sizable rivers carry the waters from the snowfields both north and south.

South of the Brooks Range lies the broad, sparsely populated Interior Basin. Through this basin flow such large rivers as the

Yukon and the Kuskokwim. The only large center of population within the Interior Basin is Fairbanks.

Then, to the south of the Interior Basin lies the Pacific mountain system, the most varied and scenic section of the state, reaching from the tip of southeastern Alaska to the end of the Aleutians. Within this system stand the Chugach Mountains, Kenai Mountains, Talkeetna Range, St. Elias Range, Alaska Range, the Wrangell Mountains, and the Aleutian Chain.

Climate

This east-west direction of Alaska's two great mountain ranges, the Pacific mountain system and the Brooks Range, is one of the major features helping to determine her variety of climates and the distribution of her people. In addition, three sides of the state face the oceans.

Along the coast of southeast Alaska the mean annual precipitation ranges up to 220 inches a year. At the other extreme, much of the north coast is an Arctic desert. The annual precipitation at Point Barrow is only four inches. Flying across this coastal plain in spring or summer, one can gain a false impression of the water resources because permafrost holds all water close to the surface.

Such differences in rainfall result from the location of the mountain ranges and the nature of the two oceans as sources of moisture. The Arctic Ocean, with its long months of ice cover and cold winds, is a poor source of moisture. The Pacific Ocean, meanwhile, with the warm Japan Current sweeping northward along the coast of southeast Alaska, provides abundant water to be carried inland on the warmer air.

This moisture falls first on the hemlock and Sitka spruce forests on the seaward side of the slopes. Here the mountains of the Pacific mountain system run largely north and south. Therefore, by the time the winds rise, cool, and pass over the towering ranges, they have already lost most of their moisture.

The Aleutians, a largely submarine range of mountains, cut off the Japan Current. The result is that the influence of the Arctic extends southward along the west coast into Bristol Bay. After studying these maritime influences on the climate of Alaska, climatologist C. E. Watson divided the state into four main climatic zones. In the Arctic Zone across the northern portion of the state, the ocean has little influence on climate except during the brief summer. Inland, the Continental Zone is a region of wide variation in temperatures. There are summer days in which the thermometer at Fort Yukon, far inland and eight miles north of the Arctic Circle, registers 100 degrees. Winter temperatures there have been known to go to 70 below zero.

The Transitional Zone, as outlined by Watson, embraces the area where much of the state's human population lives, including Anchorage, Bethel, and territory to the north along the coast beyond Nome. The fourth zone, the Maritime, is a coastal region of high precipitation, where weather is often foggy or cloudy, and where there is seldom freezing weather at sea level.

People

During the age of the Wisconsin glacier, when ice locked up a large portion of the earth's water, sea level is believed to have been some 300 feet lower than it is today. This exposed a land bridge between

A quiet stream in Tongass National Forest.
Alaska Pictorial Service

Siberia and the North American continent. Across this Bering-Chukchi land bridge came the first men to set foot in North America. They came a few at a time over the ages, perhaps seeking new hunting grounds or fishing waters.

These little bands of people established themselves in ancient outposts along the oceans. But eventually some moved inland too, and with the isolation between peoples and the passage of time, differing cultures developed. By the time Vitus Bering arrived in the Aleutians in 1741, thus becoming the first modern explorer to find this land, the native people had developed four distinct cultures.

Along the Aleutian Islands and the Alaska Peninsula live the Aleuts, the smallest native group, descended from a southern branch of the Eskimo people. The Eskimos live in the tundra country along the sea coast around the northern and western sides of the state. In southeastern Alaska the coastal people belong to three groups of Indians — the Tsimshian, Tlingit, and Haida. A fourth group are northern Indians, the Athapaskans, whose land extends from the forests of northern Canada to the Arctic.

Over thousands of years, these Stone Age people survived on the wild resources of the land and water and reached an estimated population of 74,000 — a figure believed to have been close to the carrying capacity of Alaska under Stone Age limitations. If this seems a small human population in a land with such a wealth of wildlife and fish resources, the answer may lie in the fact that people, especially those living beyond Alaskan borders, frequently have an exaggerated impression of this north country's productivity in fish and wildlife. There are places and times in which there is local abundance of game, large and small. But there are regions of Alaska, sometimes broad expanses, devoid of much sign of life. Growth rates of vegetation are slow, and the productivity of the land in animal

Eskimo hunters drag their catch, a pair of seals, to a waiting boat. *Alaska Pictorial Service* resources is tied to its ability to produce vegetation at the base of the food chain.

When fur-hungry explorers found the Stone Age culture, they brought trouble in large doses. They arrived first from Russia and later from the United States, carrying such gifts as smallpox, tuberculosis, and influenza.

Within a century after Vitus Bering's arrival, Alaska's native population dropped to an estimated 39,000. By 1950, it was down to 34,000, or half what it had been in prehistoric times. Aid of various kinds, especially medical attention, has extended the life expectancy of Alaska's native people somewhat and rebuilt her population to a level of approximately 53,000. Recent studies show the rate of population growth among natives to be about twice the national average, and of these, slightly more than half are Eskimos living in villages from Bristol Bay northward around the Arctic coast.

According to a recent study of the Federal Field Committee for Development Planning in Alaska, about 70 percent of the state's native population still live in some 178 villages where they depend heavily on the harvest of wild fish and game for subsistence. They live in places such as Minto, Kotzebue, and Sleetmute. Most such villages have fewer than 500 people, and some have only a few families. Of all these native villages fewer than a dozen are on roads of any kind. Two are along the Alaska Railroad. The remainder are reached by air, boat, dog teams, or snowmobile. Two settlements can be reached only by boat. Forty-five are without air strips, and a number of those serviced by planes cannot be reached by aircraft during the lengthy periods of spring breakup or fall freezeup. Most homes, however, have radios providing a link with the world outside and each other.

Although the natives live in a wide variety of climates, and in landscapes of magnificent variety, they share a common poverty level. One 1967 study revealed that non-native Alaskans had average incomes of $3629 per person annually, while native people averaged $600. Nor does the answer seem to be for the native people to move to the population centers, where about a third of them now live. In the cities they may earn more than their cousins back in the villages, but because of the high cost of commodities in Alaska, they often live in even greater poverty than those in their native villages.

Alaska's total population by 1970 was figured at about 285,000 people. Sixty percent of them live in and around Anchorage, the metropolis of the north. Anchorage was established in 1914 at the head of Cook Inlet as the site of the headquarters and major rail yards for the newly authorized Alaska Railroad. Later came military bases and a growing business district until today the city has tall hotels and office buildings, parking meters along its well-paved streets, and all the other marks of the modern city, including noise and automobile fumes. What it lacks in history it compensates for in robust business spirit. Anchorage is the banking and financial center of Alaska. Here men from Houston and elsewhere make million-dollar decisions about how best (most quickly) to exploit the state's remaining natural resources.

The other two major population centers of Alaska, Juneau and Fairbanks, owe their locations to gold strikes. Fairbanks, population 45,000, is a rough-hewn city in the heart of Alaska. Located as it is on the flood plain of the Tanana, a tributary of the Yukon River, this jumping-off place to the far north is sometimes plagued by serious floods. There are winter days during which it is choked by air pollution. The core of the city is modern and impressive but the outlying areas are frequently shabby and run-down. Recent years have brought feverish activity to Fairbanks. Freight-hauling aircraft roar in and out of her airport shuttling men and materials to the North Slope oil fields. New buildings reflect the boom-town flavor. So do the shortage of lodging and the $35-per-night rates on rooms.

Juneau, capital of Alaska, in the panhandle of the southeast, traces her history to 1880, when prospectors Joe Juneau and Dick Harris were scratching for gold in the gravel bed of a stream, later named "Gold Creek." Following their discovery, this place, pinched into the narrow strip of land between the mountain slopes and the sea, became a boom town.

Word of gold discovered in the Juneau area flashed southward, and soon the hopeful were headed north. Elsewhere in Alaska new strikes were made. Gold was found in the interior of the state, Nome on the Arctic coast, and the Klondike across in the Yukon Territory. Interest in the North Country grew. People came; some stayed. Others wandered south again, disappointed. Of those who stayed, some worked in the developing salmon industry.

When World War II came, federal money poured into Alaska. The U.S. Army Corps of Engineers, in a period of eight months, rammed the Alaska Highway through from Dawson City, British Columbia, to Fairbanks.

The city of Juneau exists today largely because of the government work centered there. But evidence of the gold rush still remains. Standing out against the mountainside above the city of Juneau are the massive buildings of the Alaska-Juneau gold mine. They have stood silent and empty since 1944 when the mine closed. Still locked in those hills are great stores of gold which, at current prices, cannot be mined economically.

With the new interest in Alaska, native people began receiving added assistance and a new level in health care was reached. The

In winter Fairbanks has severe air pollution caused by natural weather conditions, aggravated by man's pollutants. *Alaska Pictorial Service*

results are reflected in the fact that the population growth among Alaska's native people is now one of the highest in the world. At the time of the 1960 census, the rate of increase was greater among native Alaskan populations than it was for Mexico. The Arctic is having its own population explosion, although recent indications are that family planning is beginning to reduce the rate.

Today's non-native Alaskans trace their ancestry from many countries around the world. Alaska has the nation's youngest population, with fifteen percent of its people under the age of five, and an average age of 23 throughout the state. Half or more of its people, including a larger portion of the military personnel, live along the 50-mile-wide rail belt from Seward to Fairbanks. Much of the remainder of Alaska, in spite of scattered villages of hunters and fishermen, is wilderness country that is seldom visited.

Transportation

Because of her vast size, the nature of her terrain, and the low human population, Alaska has never developed a large system of highways. Not until World War II was there much need for roads. The total population in 1939 was about 72,000, with Fairbanks and Anchorage claiming populations of only 3500 people each. Anchorage, Fairbanks, Juneau, and Ketchikan, as Dr. George Rogers, Professor of Economics at the University of Alaska, has explained, "stand like islands." Between them stretch great mileages of water, tundra, and mountains.

Before Alaska became a state in 1958, there were 5196 miles of roads, some no more than unpaved trails. But statehood, which brought Alaska road-building funds up to about $40 million a year, did not extend the highways into the remote areas of the state. Instead, as Dr. Rogers has noted, much of the money was used to upgrade the older roads. For this is where the people live — in and around the centers of population — and the grease has gone where the wheels squeak the loudest. Today the total length of Alaska's highways is no greater than it was in 1958, and through much of the wild country across the state there seems little reason to advocate or build new highways.

Alaskans have long since found in the airplane one answer to their isolation. Bush pilots stitch the North Country together. They fly out the sick and injured, and shuttle groceries, household supplies, tools, prospectors, and scientific parties back and forth over routes that otherwise cannot be reached.

In a sense, aviation in Alaska began on July 4, 1914. That year, according to the University of Alaska's *Review of Business and*

Barrow village, the northernmost point of Alaska. *Laurence Lowry*

Economic Conditions, a group of Fairbanks businessmen arranged for daredevil pilot Jim Martin to bring his flying machine to the north. For nine minutes, Martin flew around the city, somewhat higher than the buildings, and although he did not bring his sponsors a financial bonanza, he did set the stage for a long line of historic northern fliers. By 1924, Alaska had its first airmail service with a flight between Fairbanks and McGrath. The trip that had required three weeks by dog sled was covered in a few hours by air. Air travel grew, and in Alaska today one out of every 55 persons holds a pilot's license. Wherever you care to fly, there is probably an airstrip on which you can land if you are on wheels, or a lake if your plane is float equipped. In winter most of Alaska is a landing field for planes on skis. Hood Lake, on the edge of Anchorage, is rimmed with float-equipped light planes and is the largest float-plane base in the world. The average Alaskan is as casual about flying in a bush plane as people elsewhere are about stepping into an automobile. Small planes can be hired almost anywhere. Also, the airport in Anchorage is one of the country's most important centers of international flights.

The Alaska Railroad, authorized by Congress in 1914 and completed in 1923, stretches 482 miles from the ice-free port at Seward inland through Anchorage to Fairbanks. The engineer will stop the train either to permit hunters, trappers, or prospectors to disembark into the wilderness, or to pick up homesteaders headed for town. The first cars and engines to run on this line were old vehicles that had served during the building of the Panama Canal, and for many years they swayed and bucked uncertainly along the tracks, frequently having their right of way contested by a recalcitrant moose.

Although the railroad still covers the same route, the equipment has been almost completely updated since the beginning of World War II. The Alaska Railroad, owned by the United States, is a self-supporting operation. As economists have pointed out, the building of the Alaska Railroad, contrary to the expectations of its early advocates, failed to bring many settlers or business enterprises into the regions it penetrated. Instead, the passage of years and the coming of a major war were required for human developments to catch up with the rail facilities. More recently, there have been pleas to send still another pioneer-type railroad northward on the Arctic Slope, and again the lure has been the questionable promise that such a railroad would surely "open up" the land to development.

One recent link in the Alaska transportation system is the Alaska Marine Highway, a fleet of state-owned ferry boats hauling vehicles and passengers along the scenic Inside Passage of southeastern Alaska. This system was started to promote tourism, one of the booming industries in the 49th state. And the ferry boats succeeded in doing precisely what they were launched for. Today, traveling families, many of them with motor coaches or camping trailers of wide variety, go aboard the boats with their vehicles, and for a few days travel free of the dust and tedium of the Alaska Highway. They ride at sea level among the islands and fjords where towering forested mountains rise above them. The first boats put into service along this water route carry 500 passengers and 108 automobiles over a protected 500-mile water route. Recent additions to the fleet have extended the route southward to Seattle.

Tundra on the south slopes of the Brooks Range.
Alaska Pictorial Service

The Land

More than 95 percent of the state is federal land, and about 270 million acres, or more than two thirds of the state, still lie within the public domain managed by the Bureau of Land Management.

Fortunately, lands have been set aside for the welfare of wildlife, and the U.S. Bureau of Sport Fisheries and Wildlife manages eighteen such refuge areas ranging in size from a 42-acre island to the Arctic National Wildlife Range, largest area in the entire refuge system. This is a little-disturbed Arctic wilderness of 8,900,000 acres in the northeast corner of the state. On Alaska's refuge lands live concentrations of waterfowl, sea otters, musk oxen, caribou, walruses, seals, and eagles, along with practically every other wild species known to the state.

Another major public land administrator in Alaska is the U.S. Forest Service, with jurisdiction over mountains and timberlands that total 20 million acres. The Tongass National Forest, largest of all our national forests, covers much of southeast Alaska. The remaining forest lands are found in the Chugach National Forest around the southern portion of the state and extending onto the Kenai Peninsula.

In addition to these coastal forests, Alaska has more than 100 million acres of softwood forests of spruce, birch, aspen, and poplar, growing along the major river valleys and administered as part of the holdings of the Bureau of Land Management. Totaled, the Alaska timberlands make up sixteen percent of the forest lands of the United States, an area equal to the timberlands of California, Washington, Oregon, and Montana combined. Though these states to the south have timber of higher quality than Alaska, her timber resources cover vast acreages and hold major economic promise for the developing state.

Any summer day, along the highway out of Anchorage toward Fairbanks, a considerable percentage of the drivers are seen traveling with their families in camper-type vehicles. Eventually most of them will arrive at the entrance of Mount McKinley National Park. There they will drive the park's single highway across 86 miles of unpaved road to the campgrounds at Wonder Lake. And along the way, with average good fortune, they will encounter foxes, caribou, Dall sheep, eagles, and perhaps even grizzly bears and wolves. And with better luck yet they will have skies clear enough to show them the gleaming white peak of North America's highest mountain, towering 20,320 feet into the cold blue sky. This largest of all our national parks, established in 1917, covers 1,939,493 acres of Alaska.

Following this park in rank are the nation's second and third largest National Park Service areas, also in Alaska — Glacier Bay National Monument and Katmai National Monument. In spite of their grand size, Alaska's national parks and monuments cover less than two percent of the state.

Other federal holdings include 4,100,000 acres administered by the Bureau of Indian Affairs, 23,000,000 acres of the North Slope held in petroleum reserves by the U.S. Department of the Navy, and about nine million acres set aside in 1965 as a waterpower site for the quiescent but unforgotten Rampart Dam. Roughly half of all the land still owned by the United States government is in Alaska.

With statehood, Alaska was granted rights to select about 103,000,000 acres of federal lands, by far the largest acreages ever granted a new state by the federal government. In addition it inherited its offshore lands. The Statehood Act gave Alaska 25 years within which it could select lands. Understandably, some of the earliest chosen were those of the North Slope believed to be rich in oil reserves. These have since become the site, around Prudhoe Bay, of one of the world's largest oil strikes.

But hanging over final decisions on ownership of Alaska's public lands was the long-postponed question of what to do about the land claims of the native people. As development proceeded, native organizations countered with their own claims, and because some of their claims overlapped, the total lands claimed by native groups actually exceeded the land mass of the state. Pending possible

Mount McKinley.
*Alaska Pictorial
Service*

Congressional settlement of these questions, Secretary of the Interior Stewart L. Udall in 1965 clamped a five-year freeze order on Alaska lands. Either the matter could be settled thereafter by Congressional action, or the cases would drag through the court, one by one, over the decades. By 1969, a bill aimed at settling the Alaska native claims, by outright grants of land and funds, had started its tortuous trip through the Congressional mills.

There is variety in Alaska's mineral wealth ranging from vast beds of coal to copper, lead, marble, zinc, manganese, sulphur, and several more. But today the glamour resource of the mineral group is oil, buried in hidden reservoirs beneath the state's surface in quantities that only recently have been comprehended. The conservation problems accompanying the location and removal of this high-valued resource constitute a major threat to Alaska's environment.

Since the earliest days of human occupancy by ancient Stone Age natives, Alaska's variety of fish and wildlife has been essential to the welfare of her people. The salmon industry became a major block in the foundation of the economic health of this northern region. The wildlife no longer stands between the state's human populations and starvation as it once did, but these wild renewable resources are still of vital importance to the future of Alaska.

As important parts of the wilderness, the wandering caribou, loping wolf, and fat grizzly bear belong in the picture. The broad, wet nesting grounds of the deltas draw visitors to study the waterfowl that send renewed populations south year after year. The deer of the southern forests and the caribou of the north country still supply tonnages of meat for the consumption of human beings, native and non-native alike.

Once you have traveled long enough around this state, you understand that pictures of boundless herds of wild creatures are overdrawn. Alaska does have abundant wildlife, though it should be remembered that there are broad areas of the state with little sign of life. In addition, there are seasons during which the wild creatures may be absent where they were abundant a few months before.

In any land, life begins with the soil and climate that determine the nature and abundance of its vegetation. The animal life, in turn, can only rise from the world of plants that capture, convert, and store the energy of the sun. In Alaska the climate is harsh, the growing seasons usually short, and the soil thin and frequently infertile. Where living organisms appear in abundance, especially in the cold climates, they have often accumulated over long periods of time.

Brown bears at a cascade during the salmon runs. *Alaska Pictorial Service*

The lichens on which the caribou subsist do not mature in less than a quarter of a century; arctic char grow but a few ounces a year; and the caribou, unlike some species of southern deer, seldom have twin fawns. Wilderness protection, and an understanding of the limits on the productivity of the ecosystems, are vital to the continued welfare of any natural setting.

From the Aleutians, with sea otters bobbing in the dark waters, to the home of walruses, moose, or giant brown bears, these northern lands will serve a need and fill a longing for wild scenes as wilderness grows increasingly rare. Alaska, without its natural, untamed occupants, will not be the Alaskan wilderness, and should this last frontier state lose a substantial part of its marvelous display of wildlife, she will have sacrificed one of her great promises for future income.

2

How Big Is Alaska?

ONE SUNNY MORNING two of us flew out of Anchorage and banked our small plane westward toward Bethel. Beneath us unrolled miles of marshes, brooks, rivers, odd-shaped ponds, and scattered stands of spruce and birch with a backdrop of snow-capped peaks. The wilderness stretched in every direction, and it seemed to have suffered little visible change at the hands of man. There were no roadways, villages, power lines, or smoke plumes.

This is the big Alaska, America's last great frontier. Some view it as an unlimited reservoir of wealth at the rainbow's end, too big to be hurt. "Two and a quarter times the size of Texas," one state worker in Juneau told me, "and only a quarter of a million people. Surely there is space enough to accommodate everyone."

This sprawling and varied empire has the smallest population of any state. Rhode Island has three times as many people as Alaska.

Her great reaches of open space, wealth of fish and wildlife, stores of mineral riches not yet surveyed, and a freedom from the stress of crowds — all recommend Alaska to the adventuresome. Economically, the hulking infant is just beginning to walk. When Alaska gained statehood with the act of 1958, she was beset with serious money problems. Her federal revenues were diminishing. Huge expenditures by the military had been cut back. Understandably, her leaders saw hope for the future in developing her natural resources, gaining more people, new industries, and new and larger centers of population.

What happens in Alaska is more than a simple question of States' rights. It is the rightful concern of every American. Sixty-four percent of the public land still held by the Bureau of Land Management is in Alaska, along with 85 percent of all lands administered by the Bureau of Indian Affairs, 70 percent of all the national wildlife refuge lands, 11 percent of our national forest holdings, and 31 percent of the lands administered by the National Park Service.

In his Juneau office, the U.S. Forest Service's assistant regional supervisor, George F. Roskie, a career Forest Service worker, spoke of changes that can come to Alaska. In 1946 Roskie left his Montana post with the Forest Service. When he returned fifteen years later the population growth of that state, the human invasion of once wild areas, startled him. "When I came back here in 1960, I said, 'brace your feet, the people are coming.' They couldn't believe me. It may take a while in Alaska. But it can happen."

Alaska, Roskie thinks, holds a fatal attraction. He sees in the state the promise of a "tremendous future for hunting, fishing, and camping, and especially for people to come and look at the beautiful and spectacular scenery

"Some people," he noted, "see no harm in anything that will bring more people to Alaska. They feel this will not upset things. But after seeing how much Montana has changed, I realize that it is an insidious thing. The biggest thing we can do for Alaska is manage the land so we maintain its wilderness character and still utilize the resources. This calls for the ultimate expertise."

In an earlier age, exploiters and developers could have marched across the Alaskan scene with no one raising a hand. Many seek to follow the same course today. But now there are sharp differences of thinking about how the state should manage her minerals, timber, land, water, wildlife, and scenery.

No one is saying that Alaska should not be developed, that her resources should not be tapped. There is no denying the need to build the state's economy on her resource base. It is neither practical nor possible to retain Alaska as one great wilderness region. And it is even difficult to find fault with the politician's sense of urgency, as typified by the statement from then Governor Walter J. Hickel that "the people of Alaska have twiddled their thumbs too long . . . Alaska is entering a period of change, change fostered by economic developments based on utilization of Alaska's vast stores of natural resources."

Timber, oil, and hard-rock minerals in particular are attracting vigorous and determined efforts to move Alaskan resources into commercial channels. Crews scour the wild parts of the state in search of lead, copper, gold, nickel, tin, mercury, platinum, rock phosphate, oil, oil shale, and coal. On every front the scramble gains momentum, cheered on by the political leaders who, in the eyes of conservationists, often speak too much of economic exploitation and too seldom of long-range planning. Among the conservationists the cause of concern is not so much the use of Alaska's natural resources as it is a fear that the whole economic-development rush is racing ahead with inadequate planning.

Many thoughtful Alaskans feel that this will lead their new state to repeat errors made in other parts of the country. "They say they're not going to make the same mistakes made in the Lower Forty-eight," I was told in Juneau by one concerned state worker, "but as soon as that green dollar shows up they're ready to make them."

Already there is serious pollution as sewage pours into bays and estuaries, and oil damages wildlife and aquatic resources. There is air pollution over Alaskan pulp mills and cities, strip mining in her mineral fields, and threats to her wildlife. All these hoist warning flags.

Juneau attorney Douglas L. Gregg believes that the "face of Alaska could change drastically in the next fifteen years. What may have taken fifty years in the state of Washington," he told me, "could easily be accomplished here in ten or fifteen years." He spoke of the sewage pouring into Juneau's Gastineau Channel, where he swam as a boy. Today it has been condemned as unsafe.

"Although Alaska is rich and seemingly overrun with fish, game, timber, clean fresh water, and unpolluted air, none of these resources is immune," he said. "We must have rigidly enforced laws to cope with the problem. We need them now—before the real expansion arrives, when Alaska's population may jump overnight to a million or more."

Those who insist that Alaska is too big to damage by unwise management are unrealistic. With our modern technology we have a staggering capability for misuse of natural resources. We are a people of proven ability to destroy natural wealth. We managed to turn Lake Erie, one of the world's largest natural lakes, into a cesspool. We have proved that we can tear off the tops of mountains in our search for coal, scalp forests, destroy the wilderness, lead dozens of wild species to extinction and near-extinction. We are talking of people who proved they could turn some of the world's greatest rivers into prime habitat for sludgeworms and rat-tailed maggots. Alaska's concerned conservationists realize that not only can we bruise and scar Alaska for all time, but we can also do it

The earth being washed away for placer gold at Sheep Creek near Fairbanks. *William W. Bacon III*

faster today than ever before. Alaska already has examples enough to cause deep concern among her conservation leaders.

As one conservationist who is also a Juneau attorney said to me, "The time to start doing something to protect Alaska from the kind of devastation experienced in the other states has already arrived. And full-scale industrial expansion has not yet really commenced."

"The beautiful Mendenhall Valley," he continued, "now has a population of about 7500 people as against perhaps 500 to 1000 fifteen years ago. There is no water system to serve this expanding community and water is taken from wells. There is no sewage system, and consequently each homeowner installs a cesspool. The area is now saturated with cesspools."

Fortunately, Alaska's conservationists are already organized. One organization in particular, the Alaska Conservation Society, has become Alaska's conscience regarding the handling of natural resources. With 450 members scattered about the state, the outspoken society makes its effective voice heard on matters ranging from the musk ox to copper mining. New trouble spots pop up on the map of Alaska so frequently that the conservationists are fighting endless battles urging politicians and developers to temper their exploitation with long-term thinking and planning.

"We organized in nineteen-sixty to fight Project Chariot," Ginny Hill Wood, a leader in the Alaska Conservation Society, told me. This Atomic Energy Commission plan would have opened a new harbor on the coast of northwestern Alaska with an atomic blast. "We stopped that one," I was told, "but there have been new problems ever since." Typical was the Rampart Dam affair, which is still far from dead in the minds of many of its leading promoters.

This is the project the U.S. Army Corps of Engineers referred to as "the big one," because it would have brought to the wilderness valley of the Yukon River a vast, desolate inland sea bigger than

Lake Erie. It would have drowned some of the continent's most productive wildlife lands.

The 1800-mile-long Yukon, rising in the mountains of the Yukon Territory, sweeps across central Alaska to empty into the Bering Sea. In the heart of the Yukon Valley it flows back and forth across the Yukon Flats, which are sometimes 80 miles wide. As it changes its course with floods and spring ice floes, it leaves new oxbow lakes behind and scalps old stands of vegetation, setting the stage for new plant successions to begin. It is an ever-changing, viable ecosystem, home of some 12,000 moose, 10,000 nesting sandhill cranes, 10,000 geese, and the nursery for a million young ducks a year — more waterfowl than are produced on all the national wildlife refuges combined.

But the natural contours of this valley eventually force the river into a narrowing canyon, a logical site for a huge concrete dam. Such locations are not often overlooked — even in the Arctic. In the name of economic progress, the voice of the concrete mixer was heard in the land. The construction would have spanned a decade (and the reservoir would not have filled for 20 more years) at a cost of at least $1.2 billion. Within 30 years the new hydroelectric plant would have been in full production. But by 1968 one half of all the new power plants being planned in North America were already being designed for nuclear power. Meanwhile, studies have shown that more economical power plants could be constructed in Alaska, closer to the locations where the kilowatts will be needed. Some 200 such dam sites have been inventoried in the state. Whether the cost was really $1.2 billion as the Corps estimated, or considerably higher as it was almost certain to be (even a reported $2.5 billion), it might seem sounder economy to hand the cash to Alaska outright and save the Yukon Valley.

The Yukon project got underway shortly after Alaska became a

The Yukon Flats, a rich fish and wildlife habitat, in winter. *USBCF photo by C. D. Evans*

state. Her political leaders appealed to the Senate Public Works Committee, and the Corps of Engineers was asked to investigate the possibility of a dam at Rampart Canyon. The truth is that the Corps had already explored the site and had ruled against it in interim reports as early as 1948. But by the early 1960's, under political pressure, the Corps was recommending a fresh look at Rampart Dam. The belief was advanced by politicians that we could once again pull ahead of Russia in the hydroelectric race — head her off at the Rampart. The lure of this patriotic approach is scarcely to be discounted. We were about to unleash the Engineers in the Yukon Valley.

Then came the conservationists into the picture. Dr. Ira N. Gabrielson, president of the Wildlife Management Institute, spoke out against the plan in 1963. Others joined in. Conservation organizations across the United States, including the National Audubon Society, took strong stands against the scheme. The Natural Resources Council of America sent a study team to Alaska during two summers to investigate the project, and the resulting report was a blow to Rampart Dam. Then in 1967 Secretary of the Interior Stewart L. Udall gave the plan its greatest setback when he recommended against it. Sacrificed, said the Interior report, would be a highly productive part of the continent that benefits the whole of North America at no cost.

Former Alaska Senator Ernest Gruening, later defeated, blamed "conservation extremists" for the demise of the Rampart scheme, and openly predicted that the idea would outlive those who stood in its way — specifically the Secretary of the Interior. As late as 1968 he restated his faith in the eventual building of the big dam across the Yukon. And Alaska's ex-Governor Walter J. Hickel, who succeeded Udall as Secretary of the Interior, told me about the same time that he, too, considered the idea to have merit and indicated that Rampart was far from dead. He did feel that "It will take work to convince conservationists that Rampart is really not bad for wildlife."

Meanwhile, strip mining, the scourge of the Appalachians, has become a growing threat to wild Alaska. By 1965, 11,100 acres had been "disturbed" by surface mining, 8600 acres of it in recovering gold. The current low price of gold has slowed that industry to a snail's pace, but a change in the price structure of the mineral, which some Alaskans feel is only a matter of time, could revitalize surface mining and gold dredging.

And Alaska sees a big future in its coal. "We have billions of tons of coal," I was assured in Juneau by the late Tom LaFollette of the Alaska Department of Economic Development. "Japanese firms are looking very closely at our coal."

They are looking first of all at coal fields in the Cordova vicinity, where the mineral can be recovered by strip mining. There are known coal deposits in the Palmer and Fairbanks areas. There are also extensive fields of coking-grade coal beneath the tundra south of Point Lay. In this cold land, however, one of the problems would be transporting the coal to the outside world. Some think of doing the job with trains. Others believe it can eventually be transported in huge submarine tankers which would travel beneath the ice cap to European markets.

According to the Department of the Interior's 1967 report, *Surface Mining and Our Environment*, only nine states had statutes exercising any control over the strip-mining industry or requiring reclamation measures. Alaska was not among them. This may become increasingly important as the state withdraws lands from the public domain and seeks rapid economic growth.

Currently, 50 miles east of Cordova within the Chugach National Forest, the Kortella Coal Corporation holds coal prospecting permits on 23,530 acres. Depending on whether or not a market develops for the coke, Kortella, an Alaskan corporation, intends to strip mine it, then pipe the coal as a slurry for shipment to Japan's coking industry. As the watchful Alaska Conservation Society has pointed out, this calls for an access road through the world's most important trumpeter swan breeding area, and through the nesting grounds of 10,000 to 12,000 dusky Canada geese. However, adds the society, "control over this area is much better than in most parts of Alaska." Its value as a waterfowl nesting area is thoroughly established, and the U.S. Forest Service, as well as the state's Department of Natural Resources and Department of Fish and Game, are hoping to minimize the wildlife damage.

These agencies have formally agreed to manage the Copper River delta as a waterfowl production area.

Objections to running the access road and pipeline through the wildlife-rich lands were viewed by some state workers as more obstructionist tactics. Tom LaFollette, who died recently in a crash of a bush plane, once told me, "The day of the grubstake is gone. For nine years Alaska has been a welfare state. Why not develop it fast? We want to see these resources converted into new dollars."

He harbored a monumental impatience with delays which federal agencies place in the path of all-out Alaskan development. "The act granting Alaska statehood," he explained, "carried the intent that all federal agencies were to cooperate and help the state get on its feet, but the message didn't get through to some. Some heard the words but smiled and laughed up their sleeves. I'm speaking of such agencies as the Forest Service, the Fish and Wildlife Service, and the National Park Service. We just assume that anything involving

Canada geese, molting and unable to fly. *Jack Calvin*

the federal services is trouble ahead. If the Forest Service catches you breaking a twig they get rough."

He mentioned current exploratory drilling for copper and nickel beneath Brady Glacier within Glacier Bay National Monument. When a Canadian company applied for a permit to sink an exploratory shaft within the national monument, federal agencies, as LaFollette stated it, "kept the pressure on for two years of dickering." If a satisfactory mineral deposit is found, it is assumed the company will be permitted to recover it from beneath the glacier, supposedly without disturbing the surface. "This is just an example," said LaFollette, "of how difficult and restrictive a federal agency can be to work with."

Concurrently, some Alaskans have attacked the federal government for not spending enough money to develop national park areas within the state, especially the spectacular Mount McKinley area. One group, in the interest of increased tourist development, hopes to see the building — at government expense — of a sprawling new hotel complex near the end of the Denali Highway, above the waters of Wonder Lake. For 86 miles this gravel road leads visitors deep into the spectacular wilderness of the big park. It is a fragile land where footprints on the tundra are not easily erased. It is also a great national treasure of wildlife and scenery, topped by the highest peak in North America. Large crowds of people flocking to a big commercial development at this far end of the park could only hurt the landscape and erode the wilderness experience for those who make the trip.

An alternative suggestion calls for enlarging the park to the south. From here, the hotel complex would be easily reached by the new paved highway being constructed between Fairbanks and Anchorage. Mount McKinley, the area's major tourist attraction, would still be much in evidence on clear days. The park itself and the wilderness around Wonder Lake would remain but little changed. The National Park Service has a study group exploring the various possibilities.

This threat to the unique park wilderness did not go unnoticed by the Alaska Conservation Society. When an Anchorage newspaper labeled undeveloped national parks "a truly wasted resource," Celia M. Hunter of the society wrote, "National parks and monuments were not created for the economic well-being of neighboring cities or poverty-stricken state governments. They are resources that can be prostituted and cheapened under the guise of democratically providing every mother's son his God-given right to enjoy wilderness by driving right up to the last virgin inch, where he can toss out his beer cans and lunch bags and enhance the landscape."

Disagreements have flared up frequently over the management of Alaska's vast timber resources. Long in firm control of the great timberlands of the state's southeastern section, the U.S. Forest Service has undoubtedly brought these woodlands greater protection than they would otherwise have. Most of the differences are conflicts between the Forest Service's multiple-use concepts and the desires of some Alaskans to hasten the protection of wilderness areas within the forests. The U.S. Forest Service was in business here half a century before Alaska became a state. President Theodore Roosevelt set aside the first forest lands in Alaska in 1902.

The spruce-hemlock rain forests of the Pacific Northwest extend along the coast and reach their northern limit in Alaska. Alaska has the two biggest national forests in the nation. The Tongass, covering the southeastern panhandle along the border of British Columbia, holds 16,000,000 acres. To the northwest, extending around Prince William Sound, lies Chugach National Forest. Together they blanket islands and surround fjords and harbors to include about six percent of the state's total land area.

These coastal timberlands are the home of fabled spawning runs of salmon, moving up the timber-fringed rivers. Gigantic brown bears live here. Trumpeter swans nest within the forest boundaries. Countless Sitka blacktailed deer, coyotes, giant moose, black bear, and waterfowl find their homes here.

Scattered through the Tongass National Forest, in some sixteen communities, are about 45,000 citizens. They live from the natural resources of the region: salmon fishing, timbering, and mining. Increasingly, they depend on the state's prospering tourist trade, because southeastern Alaska is both scenic and easily reached. Those coming to Alaska aboard the Alaska ferry system with their cars and

Mount Silverthrone and Wonder Lake in Mount McKinley
National Park. *Alaska Pictorial Service*

campers travel through a maze of timbered islands and secluded fjords in the shadows of spectacular mountains.

An annual 150 growing days of sixteen to eighteen hours of daylight, coupled with heavy rainfall, create dense forest growth, often with an understory of thick-growing shrubs and moss-blanketed fallen timber. As you go up the mountainsides, however, the timber thins rapidly. Three fourths of the commercial timber is said to grow within two and a half miles of the seacoast. From these forests, during World War II, huge rafts of Sitka spruce were moved southward 800 miles to Puget Sound for processing, but today timber cut in Alaska is processed at least partially within the state, a policy begun by the Forest Service years ago to protect the economy of the North.

The products of these forests are especially suitable for the pulp industry, and great blocks of the timber within the national forests have been sold to paper companies, both American and Japanese. In September 1968, U.S. Plywood-Champion Papers signed up for the biggest sale in the history of the National Forest Service — 8.75 billion board feet. In recent years, the timber production in these two national forests has climbed to more than 500 million board feet a year — up from only 60 million in 1953. And the Forest Service, pushing ahead with its multiple-purpose plans for administration of its lands, says production may still be doubled before 1980 and reach a sustained annual yield of 1.2 billion board feet by the year 2000. The question in many minds is, what sacrifices will this demand in wildlife and wilderness values?

Understandably, as both the population of Alaska and its timber harvest climb, elements of controversy could be expected. For many years the Forest Service has, as it says in one of its publications, "managed the timberlands to . . . make the greatest contribution to the territory's economy." For more than a decade its technicians have worked on details of a highly refined program of multi-use management. This plan even includes stipulations against cutting timber along certain waterways so those who travel by boat will encounter pleasing scenery.

But some Alaskan conservationists feel that the Forest Service has made these areas too small. Writing in the *Alaska Conservation Review*, Dixie Baade called these stipulations meaningless, and said that in the twelve-hour ride from Ketchikan to Wrangell you are in the no-cut zone for only half an hour.

In part, the conflict arises from the clear-cut timbering practiced in these western forests. Typically, a block of timber marked for "harvest" is cleared of all its tree cover. This, say the foresters, is the only practical way. Aside from being more economical, it is the quickest way to produce a new crop of wood. The topsoils are thin and loose and in a thin stand, trees tend to blow down. Also, the mature timber standing on areas around the clear-cut area supplies seeds that quickly (hopefully within five years) bring on a new crop of young trees. The open condition, with all areas getting full sunlight, makes for the maximum regeneration. Within 100 years the forest is ready for another harvesting.

Included in the area of the big timber sale to U.S. Plywood-Champion Papers is 100-mile-long Admiralty Island, which has been the scene of controversy for 40 years. The timber sale settles the controversy once and for all, but not to the satisfaction of those who wanted the island retained as a wilderness stronghold, a wildlife refuge, or a national park. Through the sometimes heated discussions, the Forest Service has never budged in its conviction that Admiralty is best suited to its multiple-purpose designs.

Admiralty Island covers more than a million acres and has 678

The fjord is Tracy Arm; in the distance is Admiralty Island. *U.S. Forest Service*

An adult bald eagle on Admiralty Island, one of the most productive eagle-nesting grounds in the country. *Alaska Pictorial Service*

miles of broken and scenic coastline. A chain of mountains rises to 4639 feet and forms a spine the length of the island. The mountain ridge that divides the island also separates some of the island's more famous and controversial natural resources. The finest stands of timber, according to the Forest Service, are along the western slope, the best territory for bears and salmon on the east.

This is considered the best habitat in southeastern Alaska for the big brown bears. There are believed to be 800 to 1000 of the massive brownies on Admiralty. This has brought professional guides into the stormy battle, protesting timbering on the island. The annual legal bear kill on Admiralty is about 50 animals.

Fish and Wildlife Service biologists also call Admiralty one of the most productive eagle nesting areas left in the country. A 1966 sampling showed a minimum of 443 bald eagle nests there, with a production of at least 640 preflight fledglings. At least a tenth of the young eagles raised in southeastern Alaska come from Admiralty Island.

What accounts for this concentrated population? In a word, say the biologists, "isolation." The Departments of Agriculture and Interior have established no-cut safety zones around most nest trees, but biologists still expect the increased activities to cut into the production of young eagles in one of the bird's last strongholds.

Forest Service management plans for Admiralty Island are spelled out in great detail, with provisions aimed at protection of the bears, salmon streams, and even the scenic values. Included, however, is an improved highway to extend the length of the island, as well as eventual spur roads reaching various points of interest, all contributing to the recreational development plans for Admiralty.

In reply to its critics, the Forest Service explains that only a third of the island is considered to have commercial stands of timber. In any one year of the 50-year harvest plan, the power saws will slash off only three tenths of one percent of the island. But despite the reasonable sound of this, the developments on Admiralty may spell trouble for the brown bears, because the big bears and people never have adjusted well to the presence of each other, and you cannot have your wilderness and spoil it too.

Studies so far indicate that bears return after logging crews depart. Full development of the forests for recreational use could, however, affect this picture.

In the Forest Service's view, its Admiralty plan is sound management. From an economic viewpoint, assigning top value to timber, this is true. But conservationists feel that somewhere in southeastern Alaska the future deserves a designated wilderness.

Currently there is no officially designated wilderness or primitive area within Alaska's two gigantic national forests. Says the Sitka Conservation Society, a chapter of the Alaska Conservation Society, "We face the inevitable disappearance of all natural wilderness in southeastern Alaska under present timber management plans." Some years ago the Forest Service did attempt to have the 283,000-acre Tracy Arm-Ford Terror area classified as wilderness. Mining interests, however, showed up at the hearing and shortstopped the proposal. Conceding the loss of Admiralty to the multiple-use program, the Sitka group has recently suggested to the Forest Service that the scenic and varied region of timbered islands, bays, and mountain slopes in the West Chichagof-Yakobi Island area around Sitka be designated as wilderness. This 380,000-acre area includes the recent sea otter release site in Klag Bay. It is not as well-known as Admiralty, but is considered by many to be more scenic and even better suited to wilderness designation.

Why set aside this large area in wilderness? The Sitka Conservation Society sees this as an opportunity for the American people to save a substantial and significant piece of their once vast wilderness heritage. It requires bigness, furthermore, to be a true and complete picture of what the country is like. "There must be ocean beaches, sheltered beaches, muskegs, quiet bays and lagoons, lakes, bare rocky crags. There must be an abundance of wildlife and there must be splendid virgin forest to give it shelter and to stir wonder and perhaps reverence in the minds of visitors. The West Chichagof-Yakobi country is big and splendid and beautiful. It is not too much for us to leave our children and our children's children. Indeed, considering what we started with, it is very little."

Establishing such an area as designated wilderness is more difficult than it might appear. The plan clashes with the thinking of developers such as the Juneau employee of the state's Department of Economic Development who told me happily, "All of the timber in our Tongass National Forest is spoken for." (The Forest Service puts this figure at about 60 percent.) The sources of opposition, either open or hidden, are known to the Sitka Conservation Society. "Inevitably," says its booklet proposing the wilderness, "the millmen and the loggers, whose viewpoint is understandably restricted, will cry from the housetops that maniacs are loose in the land. The bread of life is being snatched from their hands. The area is far too big — a picnic ground here and there is all that is needed. God grew those trees to be cut — not to be gawked at."

To the Sitka conservationists it seems that the Forest Service is dragging its feet in dealing with their request, which would take the area out of the timber harvest program.

The wilderness proponents sense that time is short and the years are whisking past. They see the timbering interests in full control within ten or fifteen years, and the last hope gone for balancing the landscape of southeastern Alaska with wilderness areas.

Obviously, then, there is widespread concern in Alaska over the question of wilderness designation. The subject was explored at length in a "wilderness workshop" in Juneau attended by the Forest Service and various conservation organizations. The Forest Service also asked the timber industry to cooperate and support a wilderness program. But it is still the Forest Service which must accept the primary responsibility.

In the drive to build the Alaskan economy, the timber products will assume steadily growing importance. The U.S. Forest Service is exactly the agency to put Alaska's timberlands on a sound, sustained-yield management plan. But, in the process, the call for saving some of the rain forest in true wilderness is — some insist — being smothered beneath the great blanket of multiple use.

There is also a conviction among fisheries researchers that too little is known about the effects of logging on salmon. Logging and the creation of logging roads feed sediment into salmon streams. And fisheries biologists know that sediment can reduce survival of salmon eggs and young.

During 1963 the U.S. Forest Service teamed up with the Alaska Department of Fish and Game to set up a monitoring study of such factors as sediment, water temperature, and debris in the streams from logging. But even some of the research people involved felt they were doing too little. "Monthly averages or semiannual checks," said one of the specialists at a forum on "Logging and Salmon" held in Juneau in February 1968, "do not supply information of great value when dealing with dynamics of a salmon stream."

The timber industry, which prefers to see the threat to the salmon streams soft-pedaled, forges ahead with the harvest. But there is no parallel effort to finance or organize research on the ecology of the watershed. "Unfortunately," said Forest Service fishery biologist William L. Sheridan during that forum, "there is now very little research on effects of logging on the salmon resource being conducted in Alaska."

Whether their concern is timber, minerals, water, fish, wildlife, or the whole broad ecological picture, Alaska's conservationists realize that at this early stage in her development as a state, they are already at the main junction. Right now they can make a choice. One route is the high-speed, rapid-development trail toward immediate wealth, and let the devil worry about tomorrow. Or there is the mature and somewhat more cautious path that calls for planning and careful management of the resource wealth from the beginning. As Robert E. Nelson of Ketchikan, an Admiralty lodge owner, told me, "It won't be long before Alaska, the last stronghold of natural beauty and isolation, will go the way of all scenic national parks — just one big parking lot."

As he spoke before the 1968 graduating class of the University of Alaska, Joseph H. FitzGerald, formerly chairman of the Federal Field Committee for Development Planning in Alaska, sounded a similar warning. "The development process," he said, "poses the danger that we will pollute and desecrate our lands, our forests, our streams, and the air we breathe in the same unthinking way as has been done in the older parts of the nation."

Two things are evident. First, Alaska is a big, beautiful, richly endowed, inspiring, scenic, and promising land. But man, with his modern technological capability, can cut her down to size. All he need do is attack this last frontier with his customary reckless spirit and lack of planning.

Whittling Alaska Down to Size

CONFRONTED WITH A LONG LIST of documented oil pollution cases threatening Alaska's fish and wildlife, Secretary of the Interior Stewart L. Udall early in April of 1968 issued a blunt condemnation of the manner in which Alaska's fast-growing glamour industry was neglecting its housekeeping duties. He spoke of hundreds of ducks dead from oil contamination, of fishermen's nets fouled with black crude oil, of oil-coated shellfish. The situation had brought growing concern to Alaska's wildlife workers.

The spreading of oil upon the waters of Cook Inlet is only the most dramatic of recent threats to the Alaskan landscape. Faced with an acknowledged economic need, Alaska is advancing on her oil and other resources. Alaska's leaders encourage gigantic investors to turn the eyes of the business world toward the northern frontier. The scramble is on. The prizes include tin, mercury, coal, copper, zinc, timber, oil, and other resources. Alaska's leaders see in the rapid development of these industries the promise of economic strength and growth, a burgeoning human population, and an Alaska more and more like other prosperous states.

But conservationists, including members of the thoughtful and

An aerial view of the tidal flats of Turnagain Arm
at the head of Cook Inlet. *Alaska Pictorial Service*

alert Alaska Conservation Society, continue to hoist warning flags. Alaska, they insist, despite its gigantic size is not too big to ruin. This is a land easily scarred. "Most people think this is a rugged land," James Scott of the Alaska office of the Bureau of Land Management said, "but it actually is a frail country. Destroy the living resources, and it takes three times as long to recover here as in other states."

"It is almost like telling the folks down in the Lower Forty-eight that there isn't any Santa Claus when you destroy their picture of a pristine pure Alaska by discussing our dirty water and air," says Ginny Hill Wood of College, Alaska. "We don't have any Lake Eries yet because we don't have the industrial and population concentrations to make one. But the ingredients are here — the let's-not-discourage-industry-with-too-many-restrictions attitude, and a tendency to fail to enforce the restrictions we have."

Wildlife resources, scenery, clean water, and pure air can be quickly sacrificed in the urgent rush to recover minerals and other wealth. Our early mistakes on other frontiers can be repeated. Unless the developers advance on the Alaskan scene with sound planning and under firm regulations, the last of our great frontiers is in danger. In Cook Inlet, oil is providing a dramatic and deadly example. "Nowhere else on the North American continent," said former Secretary Udall, "does the prospect of pollution from oil development pose such overwhelming threats to birds and other wildlife and to fishery resources."

Alaska conservationists trace their controversy with the oil companies from the time the industry made its first major Alaskan oil strike on the Kenai Peninsula in the summer of 1957. That was the year oil was discovered in the Swanson River area on the Kenai National Moose Range. The industrial invasion of this wildlife refuge became one of the major conservation debates of the decade. Those opposed to opening the moose refuge to oil exploration were judged guilty of what Alaska's former Senator Ernest Gruening called "unbelievably shortsighted objections."

Out of the original controversy, however, grew a system of firm guidelines and controls laid down for the oil companies by the U.S. Fish and Wildlife Service. Wildlife biologists have never been happy about the use of the refuge for oil production. On their side, the oil companies have claimed that their clearing of trails opens new areas where young growth provides abundant moose food and that, consequently, the wildlife on the Kenai is better off because the drillers came. Moose populations on the refuge are high, between 6000 and 7000 animals. And they have abundant food. But biologists know that the reason can be traced more accurately to the big 400,000-acre burn of 1947, a decade before the gates of the refuge were opened to the oil companies.

In 1964, after seven years of drilling on the refuge, the Fish and Wildlife Service completed a report which instead indicated that the oilmen were indeed inflicting damage to the Kenai sanctuary. "Although operations have been carefully controlled to minimize destructive effects," said the report, "and the oil companies have exhibited a high degree of cooperation, long-term scarring effects to the environment, the disturbance of all wildlife, pollution dangers to fisheries and waterfowl waters, increased fire hazards, and a human occupancy foreign to a natural habitat have resulted in serious detriment to the range's original objectives, invalidating earlier thoughts to the contrary."

To see what the oil industry crews would do to the refuge if left free of supervision, one need not travel far. The Swanson River field is on the east side of the Kenai Peninsula. On state lands along the

High country of the Kenai Peninsula in early morning fog. Oil companies have pushed seismic trails throughout much of this superb wilderness. *Jim Rearden*

western edge, as one wildlife worker assured me, "the oil companies went in all directions. They chewed up the landscape at will instead of restricting their travel to narrow lanes.

"They forgot their good housekeeping rules and left their garbage wherever they liked."

Supervision of the oil operations on the Kenai National Moose Range requires the full-time efforts of a professional biologist whose pay comes from the budget of the Fish and Wildlife Service. (Of the oil royalties paid by the companies working these federal lands, ten percent goes to the general federal treasury, ninety percent to the state of Alaska.)

From the Swanson River field, it was a natural extension for the oil explorers to move westward into the waters of Cook Inlet. So far, most of the oil activity there has been confined to the upper section of this huge bay. But this is only the beginning. Presently, in addition to moving farther out into Lower Cook Inlet, the oil industry is concentrating on three additional basins, the Gulf of Alaska to the southeast, biologically rich Bristol Bay across the peninsula from Cook Inlet, and far to the north, the most promising area of all, the newly discovered reserves on the North Slope of the Brooks Range, which some Alaskans feel will surely help move their state into the number-one position among the oil producers of the nation.

For five years, Atlantic Richfield Company and Humble Oil & Refining Company, working together, had poked around the tundra far beyond the Arctic Circle in search of oil. Then, two strikes in the Prudhoe Bay area during the first half of 1968 sent a wave of excitement through the entire industry and turned the eyes of investors toward the far north. Early guesses on the extent of this new strike in the Arctic ranged up to ten billion barrels, and it was described to me in Anchorage and Juneau as "one of the ten greatest oil strikes in the world." Estimates are that this new oil field could increase the North American oil reserves by a full 25 percent.

Not far to the east lies the wilderness of the vast Arctic National Wildlife Range. Three times in recent years the Department of the Interior has received requests for permits to explore for oil on the range. Each time the requests have been denied, Secretary of the Interior Udall pointing out that this fragile tundra environment is easily damaged by disturbances of any kind. The hope of those seeking the permits was that the new Secretary of the Interior would promptly open the Arctic Range to them.

There are at least ten more basins the oil industry views with promise in Alaska. To the economy of a youthful state, this is heady stuff. In 1967 mineral leases and royalties brought Alaska's treasury $13 million.

This is the kind of economic promise that leads developers to tramp roughshod over all other resources, tangible and intangible. The oil industry loses no opportunity to explain that its Alaskan operations are far more costly than those in the oil fields down south. There can be little doubt of this. They are working against a harsher environment, surrounded by higher costs of transportation and methods, and far from sources of supplies. But the oil industry is still favored by a fantastic 20 percent depletion allowance which it subtracts from profits prior to figuring its taxes. It is not a shoestring industry, and in this modern age, there is no justification for permitting it to injure the landscape permanently. Indeed, oil production costs are no greater in Alaska than in the Middle East, where a profit is made despite a 50 percent severance tax.

The oil industry likewise welcomes the lenient attitude of Alaskan politicians, as reflected in one statement by a U.S. senator there.

"We should continue to do everything to present a friendly economic, political, and social climate for this industry," he said, "bearing in mind that costs in Alaska are necessarily higher than elsewhere, and that there are plenty of other places to which the oil industry could be attracted if our favorable and receptive attitude is not maintained."

Nor is the oil industry above keeping pressure on the state to maintain this favorable attitude. The *Oil & Gas Journal,* as far back as 1961, warned Alaska through the words of the president of the Standard Oil Company of California that if oil is saddled with heavy state taxes, "you may be reasonably certain that oil money . . . will seek more hospitable climes." In truth, the idea that any oil company — today — would voluntarily pack up and leave the Alaska treasure to someone else is preposterous.

Concerned as it is with its public image, the oil industry would be well advised to learn from its Kenai experience, and take steps to protect the environment in which it works. Alaska, meanwhile, as one of her citizens suggested, might look to California, a longtime oil-producing state, for an example. Oil crews there work under rigid state control, with oil paying for the police force. As explained to me by California State Oil and Gas Supervisor Fred E. Kasline, an inspector from the California Department of Fish and Game goes along when an oil crew engages in geophysical explorations underwater. "The cost of the inspectors," he adds, "is paid by the oil company conducting the work. This added cost, while often substantial, has not hampered the development of the oil industry in any way."

This idea seems still valid despite the recent oil disaster at Santa Barbara, California. The blowout at a Union Oil Company offshore rig occurred in an area leased from the federal government and not

An oil blowout in the Kenai National Moose Range, one of the finest moose habitats in the state. *U.S. Fish and Wildlife Service*

under the jurisdiction of the state of California. Federal regulation and policing of such operations has been condemned as lax; the Interior Department had conducted no independent geological studies, relying solely on information supplied by the oil companies.

Once the oil companies began to explore in 1959 beneath the waters of Cook Inlet, that broad arm of rough water and 35-foot tides lying just to the west of the Kenai Peninsula, five companies joined forces. In the summer of 1962 one of their discovery wells struck oil. The rush was on, and the stage was set for a new conflict between oil and wildlife.

Along the mud flats of Upper Cook Inlet, where the oil platforms first appeared, ducks and other water birds feed in abundance. High tides can carry oil slicks into feeding areas in the marshes. Along the west side of Cook Inlet lies the two-mile stretch of nesting cliffs for kittiwakes, puffins, auklets, gulls, murres, guillemots, and other birds within the Tuxedni National Wildlife Refuge. These birds feed on and in the water.

Out of these waters come great quantities of the commercially valuable king crab and Dungeness crab, as well as salmon and shrimp, and a new scallop fishery, valued together in recent years at $1.5 million annually.

Across from Anchorage, along the west side of Cook Inlet, are the famed Susitna Flats, one of Alaska's most important migratory waterfowl areas, extending for more than 100 miles. "Our fear," I was told in the Anchorage office of the Fish and Wildlife Service, "is that there might be an oil line break sometime when there is also a high tide and a strong east wind. This would be a calamity during either the spring or fall migrations." In fall, such a spreading oil film might wipe out large numbers of lesser Canada geese, pintails, mallards, teal, widgeon, trumpeter and whistling swans. In spring, it could destroy most of the big flocks of snow geese that congregate here on their way north.

The drilling crews work from giant platforms that cost the oil companies from $12 to $15 million apiece. In 1968, thirteen of these platforms dotted Upper Cook Inlet. The wells are drilled through the platform legs, and oil pumped from them is forced through concrete-encased underwater pipelines to storage tanks on land, from which it is then loaded onto tankers. There are 116 miles of these pipelines, sometimes extending uninterrupted for several miles on the floor of Cook Inlet. If there is a break in one of the lines, an automatic shut-off valve at the well is expected to stop the pumps. There has sometimes been discussion about whether there are also valves spaced along the pipelines. There are not. Although the pumps at the well may stop when there is a break in the line, there is all the oil in perhaps several miles of the broken pipe to worry about. Still, Harry Morrison, vice president and general manager of the Western Oil and Gas Association, told Secretary Udall on April 1, 1968, that "Crude lines, i.e., flow lines from platforms to shore, are equipped with automatic and/or remote shutoff valves." But in August, I was told by a public information representative of the Alaska division of the Western Oil and Gas Association that "operators inform us there are no cut-off valves in these lines except at either end."

There are other ways the oil industry can and does pollute Alaska's waters.

One February day in 1968, a commercial fisherman from Seldovia, on the southern end of Alaska's Kenai Peninsula, witnessed a scene that made him fighting mad. One of the big oil tankers that regularly move in and out of Cook Inlet, transporting oil from Alaska south to California, was leaving an ominous oil slick spreading in her wake.

A pair of trumpeter swans. These still rare birds winter in ice-free Cook Inlet, vulnerable to the constant threat of oil spills. *Leonard Lee Rue III*

Turning on his radio, the fisherman contacted a State Fish and Game Department biologist, Jim Rearden, at Homer, Alaska.

On Rearden's suggestion the fisherman collected samples. Soon, Rearden flew over the ship and made aerial photographs. The ship in question was the 29,000-ton *Rebecca,* which carries a crew of 45 and has a 350,000 barrel capacity, one of the largest ships working Cook Inlet. When such ships run empty, they sometimes take water into their tanks, adding weight to make them perform better in rough seas. The ballast is later pumped into the open sea, and there may be oil with it. Increasingly touchy about instances of oil pollution threatening the fish and wildlife resources of Cook Inlet, Alaska officials were confronted here with what appeared to be a flagrant violation. The *Rebecca* was coming in to pick up a load of crude oil and was emptying her hold in preparation.

Later that evening, word of the oil slick in the inlet down at Homer reached then Governor Hickel in Juneau. He promptly went into a huddle with cabinet members, including a representative from the state attorney general's office. The state's laws controlling pollution, however, were notably weak, and the governor's problem was finding a law on which to proceed against the offending captain.

At two o'clock that night the governor called a news conference. He had reached his decision. The *Rebecca*, due in Nikiski, 100 miles south of Anchorage, that morning, would be met by a welcoming committee from the state patrol. Tests had already been run on the ballast from the ship. The state patrolman arrested the ship's captain, Elmer V. Johnson, under a federal law of 1899. Alaska at the same time seized the *Rebecca* as evidence and she was held for 36 hours amid anguished cries from her owners; after the posting of a $100,000 bond the tanker was released.

The case against the captain dramatized the need for stronger pollution laws. The following March, the state senate unanimously voted its approval of a new bill permitting confiscation of tankers polluting the waters with oil. But this move is less daring than it appears. As one Alaska conservationist said, "Strong action against tankers doesn't carry the same home-front political implications as action to stop pipeline breaks and spills from platforms and shore facilities."

Dozens of other oil pollution cases have been recorded since the oil well drilling platforms came to Cook Inlet. Commercial fishermen have brought king crabs from the deep bottom of the inlet coated with crude oil, increasing the speculation that silt drags oil to the bottom where it may threaten a delicate ecology. Oil-coated ducks have washed ashore, dead or nearly dead. And wildlife workers go about their duties aware of the constant threat of a wildlife disaster.

The actual well-drilling operations have accounted for some of the more flagrant pollution instances. The first oil to come from a new well arrives at the surface mixed with cuttings and drilling mud. These waste materials, plus perhaps another 100 barrels of crude oil, are pumped out until the oil comes pure. Often, in the past, the wastes — and the first oil — were pumped directly into the bay before the new wells were capped off for later production. During the summer and fall of 1966, inspectors from the Anchorage office of the Federal Water Pollution Control Administration recorded numerous instances of oil slicks spreading across portions of the inlet. Then during the following spring, while visiting one of the drilling platforms, a biologist was told by oilmen that such pumping of new wells directly into the bay had been common practice the summer before. "Apparently," the biologist reported to his superiors, "our eyes were not deceiving us in our patrol activities last fall, and we were certainly not told the truth about operations in the inlet by either the oil companies or by the State Division of Mines and Minerals."

So frequent did the reports of oil slicks become that even the oil companies could scarcely deny them. Waterfowl biologists surveying the inlet in December 1967 reported two areas of iridescent sheen. One slick was about 200 feet wide and half a mile long. Another appeared to be the mixture of oil and drilling mud. And reaching from the docks used by the oil-rig tender boats and stretching for three miles was another slick a quarter of a mile wide. On that day many thousands of waterfowl — perhaps 100,000 — were using the inlet.

Later the same month a tanker freshly loaded with 127,000 barrels of crude oil was caught on one of the inlet's powerful tides and rammed into a dock. A compartment was ruptured and as the tanker was towed across the inlet for unloading, 1500 barrels of oil, 63,000 gallons, spilled and spread for twenty miles.

But the most dramatic wildlife loss from oil on Cook Inlet to date occurred in November 1967. It killed an estimated 2000 waterfowl. The source never was determined. Ray Morris with the Federal Water Pollution Control Administration believed it might have been pumped from a ship moving through the inlet. It may be that the captain responsible believed he was far enough at sea that the act would not be noticed. But a storm sweeping across Cook Inlet apparently moved some of the oil-soaked ducks into plain view of shore. And according to the Department of Fish and Game, there is a colony of 50 to 75 sea otters living 75 miles southwest of Homer. Sea otters coated even with small amounts of oil may die very quickly. More difficult to measure are the losses suffered by anadromous fish in such oil-polluted waters.

As oil production in Cook Inlet climbed steadily, and the pollution problem grew increasingly serious, reports from federal investigators made their way to the desk of the Secretary of the Interior. In April 1968 he called for an emergency control program and more conscientious efforts by industry. "During recent months," Secretary Udall said, "I have received well-substantiated evidence that exploration and development activities in Cook Inlet have resulted in a recurring series of pollution incidents. Between June 1966 and December 1967," he added, "there were some 75 incidents of oil pollution in Cook Inlet reported by federal and state agencies responsible for the conservation of natural resources in the area."

One report made available to the secretary revealed that "nearly 100 oil pollution incidents have been recorded in Cook Inlet, Alaska, between March 1966 and April 1968." If an oil company's operations cause a spill, the incident is supposed to be reported promptly to the authorities, according to regulations. Sometimes it is, and other times it is kept quiet. Of the 100 cases, the report said, "Twenty-two of these oil spills were reported by the oil industry, but ten were late reports." Out of 23 spills during the first four months of 1968, only seven were reported. It was evident that the honor system had its weaknesses.

The most common causes of oil incidents have been pipeline breaks and spills from the permanent platforms. A series of aerial observations revealed that the inlet was free of "visible" pollution only 34 percent of the time. Today oil leaks into Cook Inlet almost every week and the situation is far more serious than most people realize.

There is another reason why the formation of the secretary's recommended federal task force was timely; the oil industry is preparing to spread out from the upper section of Cook Inlet into Bristol Bay, where there has been no such pollution threat to fish and wildlife.

In Bristol Bay, the wealth of wildlife is even greater than in Cook Inlet. Called by ornithologists "a crossroad" for waterfowl, Bristol Bay is used by birds returning to nesting grounds from as far away as Mexico and Japan. It is the final staging area for thousands of northbound nesting birds that move on to the Arctic each year as soon as spring has ushered in the ice breakup. And in winter, diving ducks and sea birds populate Bristol Bay by the hundreds of thousands. In short, it is an incredibly rich concentration point for North American birdlife — one of the most important in the world.

Too, along the 1500-foot cliffs stretching for 20 miles on the north side of Bristol Bay, perhaps a million sea birds crowd in to nest in

Chester Creek dumping badly polluted water into already polluted Knik Arm near Anchorage. The seawater is laden with silt from large glacial streams at the head of the arm. *Alaska Pictorial Service*

summer. The Fish and Wildlife Service admits that it has only sketchy information on the total numbers of birds relying on the waters of this bay during any year. But in its files are notes of observers recording rafts of ducks 100,000 strong. Windrows of molted wing feathers a foot and a half deep have built up for miles along the beaches.

Then there are the marine mammals — seals, sea lions, the little white beluga whales, sometimes porpoises; and at Walrus Island, the only place in the United States where walruses come ashore, some 3000 bulls live the year around.

Salmon migrating through these waters would suffer serious harm from oil pollution — and Bristol Bay is the world's greatest salmon fishing area. There have been years when about half of Alaska's salmon production has come from these waters. In 1965 — a peak year — the salmon harvest was worth $54 million wholesale. In addition to the direct harm to the fish as they migrate through the bay and near the surface, biologists know that oil can cause serious losses from contaminating the smaller organisms on which commercially important fish survive. It is little wonder that the thousands of commercial fishermen around Bristol Bay view the approach of the oil rigs with misgivings and that conservationists urge stricter laws and enforcement.

Recently, too, Collier Carbon and Chemical Corporation completed construction of a giant new $50-million plant at Nikiski, on the Kenai Peninsula, to manufacture ammonia-urea fertilizer at the rate of 1500 tons per day for shipment to Japan and to the West Coast. The problem was what to do with the chemical waste products. Collier was the first industry to seek state permission to dump its wastes into Cook Inlet. Concerned groups included the State Department of Fish and Game and the Federal Water Pollution

Control Administration. In 1968, the company operated on a temporary permit allowing it to run 820,000 gallons of waste per day into the inlet. The firm, state and federal workers, and researchers from the University of Alaska are attempting to keep careful watch on what this source of heat and chemical pollutants might do to the estuary and its fish life. And Collier, in a "guarantee that the inlet will not be harmed by our production operations," is now installing "more elaborate antipollution equipment at the Kenai plant than exists at any ammonia plant in the world." Conservationists still are not at ease about the situation, and some insist that the state was too lenient from the first in its efforts to encourage the development.

In the harbor at Sitka, scene of a bustling wood processing industry, the pulp mill practices what is known as "in-plant" pollution control. But the treated liquors are still run off into the saltwater estuary and, say local conservationists, they contaminate the water for miles around. Fishermen complain that when they return to the Sitka harbor they can no longer tie their crabs overboard and expect them to live.

In the effort to meet federal water quality standards, Alaska's municipalities are only now taking early steps toward treatment of their sewage. Cook Inlet waters around Anchorage, and bays near other communities, are badly polluted from raw sewage.

Looking northward to the icebound riches of the Arctic, Governor Hickel foresaw the need for improved transportation if the resources of the Brooks Range and the North Slope were to be tapped. He created the NORTH Commission, composed of businessmen from both Alaska and other states. "One of our first objectives is for this commission to come up with a method to build and extend the Alaska Railroad through the highly mineralized area of the Kobuk country.

With the development of these mineralized areas we will develop composite cities, create employment, and bring in royalties for the state." In Juneau, the late Tom LaFollette of the Alaska Department of Economic Development predicted that there would be both a railroad and a highway extending into the far north. And discussion of an 800-mile pipeline to bring oil from the newly discovered North Slope fields to the Gulf of Alaska south of Anchorage was just getting underway.

In December 1968 the Alaska Department of Highways bulldozed the ground vegetation off the first of more than 400 miles of winter road to extend from just north of Fairbanks to Prudhoe Bay. This temporary road, finished by February, spanned the Yukon River on a bridge of ice. It also marked what some hoped would be the first step in establishing a permanent highway into the area of the Arctic oil strikes. With the push on for rapid development of even the most remote Alaskan frontiers, there can be little doubt that people and their works will soon appear increasingly on the wilderness scene.

New communities, then, may blossom across the Alaskan Arctic. "We estimate that this type of development can, in the foreseeable future, produce a series of communities — possibly a dozen or more — across the northern part of the state, each with 5000 to 7000 people," Joseph H. FitzGerald, formerly chairman of the Federal Field Committee for Development Planning in Alaska, told a 1967 meeting at College, Alaska.

What will bring people to the far north? Largely it will be the mineral wealth of the region, including the oil. "Development in the Brooks Range," FitzGerald has said, "is the major step in opening up the interior. If the mountains are as highly mineralized as many believe, there is a potential of dozens of mines, each supporting a substantial community. Surface transportation would, in all probability, be by either an east-to-west railroad or by highway, or both. Beyond the Brooks Range lie the potentially great oil and gas fields of the Arctic Slope."

This is a region where, as one conservationist reminded me, "a footprint lasts five years."

What will the Arctic communities be like? Across Arctic Canada, and in Alaska, I have many times visited communities as far north as any likely to be constructed on Alaska's North Slope. Such communities have a frontier atmosphere. Life is harsh and the sheer force of performing the necessary tasks sometimes makes the non-essentials seem like wasted energy. There is a litterbug complex that leaves the tundra around such villages decorated with abandoned oil drums, discarded vehicles, and fallen buildings. Time will reveal whether the villages materialize. But it would be a novel and laudable development if they were planned far in advance to avoid excessive abuse to the landscape.

It is true that some efforts are being made to safeguard Alaska's tremendous resource and scenic wealth against the destruction that can come from unplanned exploitation. The U.S. Bureau of Land Management, the biggest landholding agency in the state, is moving forward with a system of land classification and is working closely with the Alaska Department of Fish and Game. It was recognition of past problems in the Lower 48 that led Congress to pass, in 1964, the Classification and Multiple Use Act, the foundation of BLM efforts to put some order in the use and disposal of its holdings.

In its 1968 session, the Alaska Legislature passed new water pollution control laws. This new legislation, known as "Chapter 109," specifically lists materials such as petroleum, acid, oil, and coal tar which the state considers pollutants in its waters. It provides for fines ranging from $500 to $25,000 and jail terms ranging from

A Sitka pulp mill pours pollution into the air. *William Garnett*

30 days to one year for offenders willfully adding such pollutants to the water. Moreover, these laws can be enforced by law officers of the State Fish and Game Department who are widely spread over the state. The same laws give the state definite authority to seize vessels polluting the waters.

But efforts to pass air pollution control laws in the same session failed. Largely, this was due to pressure from pulp mill operators in southeastern Alaska. Air pollution over the great open spaces of this gigantic state seems unimaginable to the outsider. But the state is already confronted by periodic evidence of serious atmospheric contamination. In winter, Fairbanks has a serious air pollution problem because a dome of dense, cold air shuts off the escape of car exhausts, smoke, and other pollutants. State Senator W. I. "Bob" Palmer introduced the ill-fated bill. His fellow senator, Lowell Thomas, Jr., told me, "Although it may seem premature, now is certainly the time to set up provisions for avoiding the kind of atmospheric pollution that now plagues so many other parts of the United States, and the world, for that matter. It would be foolish indeed for us to wait until we have a crisis on our hands to pass legislation that could have prevented that crisis."

It would seem equally foolish for Alaska to permit the special interests and the impatient politicians full freedom to advance against any of her resources with inadequate planning for long-range protection of the landscape. Her scenery and wildlife create a tourist industry that promises spectacular growth and economic potential — and which could suffer greatly.

As Joseph FitzGerald told a graduating class at the University of Alaska, "What is needed now is an identification of a statewide system of parks, wilderness areas, wildlife refuges, and recreational areas, a blueprint which all governments can follow as funds become available. The success of these efforts will have a more profound effect on the future of Alaska than any other development effort."

It was FitzGerald who told me in his Anchorage office, "The romance of the frontier is largely in the American mind. We don't want to bring economic development that permits history to repeat the mistakes of the frontier, and destroys the land pattern. How do we grow wisely and well and preserve the quality of life? All frontier life is a bit free-booting." FitzGerald sees Alaska as a new state operating by seat-of-the-pants judgment and says, "Ultimately, this is not good enough. We have to ask ourselves what we want Alaska to be a hundred or a thousand years from now. What is needed is a system. If we concentrate on this planning, only good can come out of it."

Alaska's political leaders and economic developers are inclined to say that Alaska is fifty years behind the times, that their new state has a lot of catching up to do. One thoughtful member of the Alaska Conservation Society, writing in that organization's *Alaska Conservation Review,* said, "We are not fifty years behind the other states. Rather, we are an eternity ahead of them. Our bank of natural resources is still nearly full — at least fifty years fuller than that of other states. Behind? Not by a long shot. And we ought not to measure Alaska in terms common to other states and what they have. The reason many of us are up here in the first place is because we don't like what they have."

Alaska has a hard core of such concerned and knowledgeable conservationists. They are her conscience. And if she heeds this conscience, Alaskans of the future will be able to say their state profited from others' mistakes and developed our last frontier with sensitivity and minimum damage to this big, unique, and exciting state.

4

Alaska's Magnificent Wildlife

ALTHOUGH IT WAS NEARLY MIDNIGHT, there was still enough light for me to work on my notes on the screened porch of the little cabin. For music I had the haunting sounds of the wilderness coming across the Minto Flats. Above the marshland, courting snipe alternately climbed and lost altitude, and breezes whistling through the birds' wings repeated a wind song — like air blowing across the mouth of a bottle.

Suddenly, the wild sounds were drowned out by some large animal crashing through the underbrush beyond the cabin and disappearing before I could catch a glimpse of it. So now I sat quietly, staring into the brush, to see if it might return. Finally a patch of cinnamon-colored fur moved, and gradually the shape of a huge bear materialized as the animal worked its way toward the opening where the cabin stood. My first thought, because of the bear's size and unusual coloring, was that a grizzly had come in search of food. But a more careful look proved that he lacked the head and shoulders of a grizzly. As I later learned, there are no grizzly bears on those flats. The visitor was a color phase of the black bear clan.

He came to the edge of the clearing and sniffed the night air,

Bull moose in velvet.
Leonard Lee Rue III

moving now with a quietness uncanny for so large an animal. Once he paused while taking a step and held one of his hind feet above the ground with just the claws touching the leaves. For several seconds he held that pose, then set that long flat foot down an inch at a time without disturbing the silence around him. And after he investigated the scraps from the kitchen, he melted again into the woods where his wild ancestral surroundings lay undisturbed and his wild neighbors were those the bears had always known.

Nearby in the swamps lived some of the world's largest moose. We had seen them dipping their long faces into the cold waters to harvest the vegetation. And in the waters of the nearby river swam both pike and sheefish. Earlier, in other parts of Alaska, we had seen the nimble-footed mountain goats and Dall sheep, wandering caribou, a feeding red fox, seals, sea otters, walrus, countless pelagic sea birds nesting on jagged rock cliffs projecting from the waves, and, farther inland, thousands of nesting waterfowl. On this northern scene you may also encounter polar bears, brown bears, and glacier bears, wolves, coyotes, and wolverines, ravens, sandhill cranes, and trumpeter swans, and five kinds of salmon in the water — a wealth of wildlife that brings to mind the accounts of early wilderness travelers from Henry Kelsey to Lewis and Clark.

This wild wealth of Alaska helps give the "Great Land" its magic. This is the fabled North Country, and its spectacular wildlife resources are both a state and a national treasure.

In Alaska, as elsewhere, the earliest settlers viewed the abundant wildlife as theirs to kill, even in excess of their needs. The musk oxen that wandered the wind-whipped tundra were wiped out by 1867. On the Kenai Peninsula, much of the lichen growth was destroyed by fire, and the caribou were mostly gone by the turn

A magnificent Dall sheep ram. *Willis Peterson*

of this century. With them went the wolves. By 1900, the sea otters were almost extinct.

Later there were bounties on eagles, seals, wolverines, coyotes, and other animals believed to compete with man for salmon, livestock, and wild game. Airplanes, then snowmobiles, shrank the vast distances. And more recently the bustling industrial activity and the

Mountain goats perched on a crag. *Leonard Lee Rue III*

promise of a greatly increased human population threaten steadily mounting pressure on Alaska's wildlife, even on some of the refuges and parklands that have been set aside over the years.

Some still view Alaska's wildlife as being in endless supply, and the sheer abundance breeds an attitude of relaxed exploitation. We may have heard about the fate of the bison on the plains to the south, the disappearance of the grizzly in the Lower 48, and the decimation of the wolves. But, if it matters at all, we are too often inclined to feel that it can't happen here.

Yet as one example, Alaska's population of magnificent brown bears is almost certain to diminish as human activity spreads. History assures us this is true. No one knows how many of the big bears live in Alaska; there have been repeated efforts to census them, but biologists have never yet worked out a sound system for such a count. The closest they can come to statistics, and it might at best indicate local trends, is data collected from guides and hunters on the numbers of brown or grizzly bears killed each year. Such figures might also reflect increased hunting pressure or changes in equipment and techniques. The total of browns and grizzlies taken by sportsmen in Alaska climbed from 473 in 1961 to 776 in 1967.

As anywhere else, the bears have found their greatest pressure from humans in areas which are near livestock operations, especially on Kodiak Island, the Kenai Peninsula, and in Matanuska Valley. Grizzly bears do kill livestock, although bear authority Dr. Albert W. Erickson, for seven years an Alaska big game biologist before moving to the University of Minnesota, believes that only a few animals develop such traits. But a grizzly seen anywhere in the vicinity of livestock is usually considered a stock-killer and is quickly dispatched. It is common enough for ranchers to claim greater damage from bears than they actually suffer, and animals lost to other causes are often credited to bears. The grizzly that finds and feeds on a carcass, leaving his tracks on the scene, adds fuel to the fire.

Cattlemen and defenders of the grizzly are on a collision course. Perhaps the most noted clash between these groups came in 1963 when, at the ranchers' request, a former fighter pilot and ex-cattle rancher, then flying for the Alaska Department of Fish and Game, began gunning down grizzlies on Kodiak Island with a semiautomatic rifle mounted World War style on top of a Piper Cub and sighted in at 150 yards. The plane's pilot, who was also president of the Kodiak Stock Growers Association, proved the efficiency of killing bears with fighter-plane techniques by eliminating thirteen of the giant creatures, some of which were said to be in the vicinity of cattle. Fish and Game authorities ordered a halt to the airborne slaughter, but the same plane had racked up a mighty record of bear killing even before the development of the ingenious gun mount. Flying with a state representative serving him as relief gunman, the pilot had already taken 22 bears earlier in the year, according to a report by a Department of Fish and Game biologist. And instead of selectively shooting only bears known to be stock-killers, the operation had been a general thinning process — with any grizzly spotted a likely victim.

Whether timbering activity on the forests of southeastern Alaska cuts into the bear populations is, according to Dr. Erickson, dependent largely on whether the operation muddies the streams and reduces the salmon population, a principal food for the bears. The degree and duration of human disturbance is also a factor. U.S. Forest Service studies indicate that although timbering operations force bears from an area, the effect is temporary.

For the big bears of Alaska, which throughout much of the state still occupy their wild lands in almost undiminished numbers, the future depends on a reasoned system of granting them refuge in some of their better natural range. National parks and refuges already offer protection on such lands as Kodiak National Wildlife Refuge, Izembek National Wildlife Range, and Mount McKinley National Park, plus the state's famous bear sanctuary on McNeil River off Cook Inlet.

The time may well come when there should be complete protection given the bears. For now, most Alaska biologists do not see the need for such action. But one problem is that the list of Alaskan bear experts includes every guide and many of the politicians in the state, and if they would put aside their prejudices and listen to the biologists, the big bears of Alaska could have a long and secure future. Thought must be given at this early stage in Alaskan exploitation as to where the bears fit into the resource management picture. If the needs of the bears are ignored or left to opposing

A humpbacked brown bear with a salmon.
Leonard Lee Rue III

An Alaska grizzly with cubs. *Charlie Ott*

political forces to settle by power and pressure, their future is indeed dim.

There is no chance whatsoever that Alaska's population of big bears will be preserved — statewide — at present levels. As pressure from development grows, the decimation will come not from the hunter as much as from industrial forces. Some reductions are both justifiable and inevitable, according to Dr. Erickson, especially in areas not best suited to bears. At the same time he has urged an early review of land use possibilities, especially on the Alaska Peninsula, to locate those areas with the greatest potential for the big brown bears. "Every attempt should be made," he adds, "to preserve these critical areas." The fear is that in area after area, as the demand for timber, oil, and other resources increases, the remaining populations of grizzly or brown bears will be pushed farther down the list of valuable natural resources. Recent oil developments on the North Slope, as one example, are certain to work to the detriment of the population of barren ground grizzlies.

The polar bear, meanwhile, mystery animal of the Arctic wilderness, is the subject of continuing controversy — and research. Nobody can be quite certain what the status of the magnificent white bear is from year to year. The worldwide annual kill is estimated at 1300 to 1400 animals. Whether the polar bear is holding its own is a secret locked in the frozen terrain the great carnivore inhabits. Distances, transportation difficulties, scattered bear populations, harsh weather, and the nature of the creature itself combine to hide the white monarch's secrets from human investigators. In recent years we have begun to learn bits of new information about polar bears, but it is a difficult struggle. Such basic information as life expectancy or the number of cubs a sow might produce during her lifetime are still deep mysteries of the polar ice pack.

Polar bears on an icepan. *National Film Board of Canada*

Biologists know that mating occurs in spring and that during this season males may roam great distances. Breeding is usually in April, according to Jack Lentfer, wildlife biologist with the Alaska Department of Fish and Game. Females have their young in icy dens, usually in November or early December, and for an animal the size of the polar bear, the newborn young are small indeed — they weigh only a few ounces. The female usually has two young, occasionally one or three. Cubs normally stay with the female until they are past two years old. It is believed that the females breed every third year.

Until recently, each country within the polar bear's range went about its research and management of the animal individually. But the ice bear is an international resource, drifting sometimes from country to country on ice floes, or traveling where he chooses overland without regard to national borders. Because of this, plus a growing fear that the polar bear might be facing serious troubles, authorities from five countries assembled in September 1965 at the University of Alaska for the first International Scientific Meeting on the Polar Bear. Present for the five-day conference were polar bear authorities from Denmark, Norway, Canada, the United States, and the Soviet Union.

Those assembled discussed cooperative efforts to study the polar bear; they were not authorized to set international agreements. Russian delegates suggested there be a worldwide halt in the hunting of polar bears for five years until the status of the animal could be determined. Estimates of the earth's total polar bear population ranged from 10,000 to 20,000 animals.

But representatives from the United States were not eager to see more stringent limitations on the annual polar bear kill on American ice. This can be traced easily to the facts of economic life in Alaska, where visiting hunters from the Lower 48 pay $2000 or more to come north and kill a white bear on a guided hunt. The bears — which are at the very peak of the Arctic food chain — face no enemy except man.

Hunting out of such northern villages as Kotzebue, Teller, Barrow, and Point Hope, visiting sportsmen employ airplanes in their pursuit of these giant bears. The usual practice is for a guide to use two airplanes flying together. Once they spot the tracks left in the snow by a traveling bear, they follow the trail until they locate their quarry. After they land on the ice, the client climbs out and, along with the guide, follows the trail for perhaps a few hundred yards until he gets into a position to pot his trophy — which the second plane has driven into position for the kill. So, a few days after leaving home, the sportsman is back down south telling about his adventure.

It is true that airborne hunters do select trophy animals instead of the smaller producing females — especially if they are traveling with responsible guides. But this type of bear hunting has led to bitter discussions of what really constitutes sportsmanship. In 1966 the one million-member National Rifle Association announced it would no longer offer big game hunters its award for polar bears if taken with the aid of aircraft. And the venerable Boone and Crockett Club of New York City removed the polar bear from the list of animals eligible in its big game competitions. Then in 1967 the Alaska Board of Fish and Game issued new hunting regulations that restricted still further the kill of polar bears.

Meanwhile in another and certainly less controversial brand of hunting, research specialists from both the U.S. Fish and Wildlife Service and the Alaska Department of Fish and Game have been locating and capturing polar bears with the aid of aircraft. They overtake the bears with helicopters, immobilize them with chemicals, and after recording data about each bear captured — and marking

A bull seal with his harem and pups. The cold Bering Sea
is surprisingly rich in wildlife. *Alaska Pictorial Service*

it for later identification — release the groggy giants. During 1968,
142 polar bears were captured and marked in Alaska in an effort
to answer some of the unsolved riddles of the big bruins.

Critics of restrictions on polar bear hunting frequently say there
is no proof the polar bear is in trouble. But faced with the fact that
most questions about their status remain unanswered, it is reasonable
to argue that the great white bears deserve the benefit of the doubt.
Conservative regulations seem in order until we understand the bears
better and know what protection they must have if they are to stay
off the world's list of endangered species.

There is evidence, meanwhile, that the fish and marine mammals
of the far north will suffer increasingly as human pressures build.

The outlook for the salmon industry, long the biggest income producer on the Alaskan scene, is cause for grave concern. Enough adult salmon must swim back up their ancestral streams to spawn and maintain the population. And there is widespread conviction that the highly efficient Japanese fishing vessels are taking more than the safe harvest from the adult populations in international waters.

Overharvesting by both American and foreign fishermen has caused the collapse of the king crab industry. Now there is a newly developing scallop industry, and observers already wonder if overfishing will quickly diminish this resource as well. The fact is evident that in these cold northern waters, wild creatures — although abundant — do not grow as rapidly as in warmer regions.

There is also concern among biologists for certain of the marine mammals inhabiting Alaskan waters. The walrus is frequently a victim of wasteful hunting. One study by Fish and Game Department biologists yielded the observation that poor hunting methods wasted at least half of the walruses killed by native hunters. Government-sponsored native craft programs have encouraged ivory hunting, with the result that a 3000-pound bull walrus may be killed for a dozen pounds of ivory tusks, and the meat left to waste.

During its 1968 meeting at Fort Collins, Colorado, the American Society of Mammalogists took notice of the plight of the walrus and ribbon seal. Together, Soviet and American hunters annually take some 30,000 seals. For the Eskimos this is primarily subsistence hunting, and has long been practiced. But beginning in 1962, the Soviets added highly efficient commercial sealing vessels to the picture and increased the kill by 50 percent or more, mostly ribbon seals. This was enough to cause concern among both Soviet and American ecologists for the future of the species, and the American Society of Mammalogists has called for international agreements

Walrus on
Round Island.
*Alaska Pictor-
ial Service*

designed to guard both seals and walruses against any overhunting which could threaten their survival.

Among the stranger dramas these days on Alaska's wild scene is the hassle over the musk ox. This shaggy, heavy-horned creature of the Arctic barrens has long since been eliminated from its native Alaska range by overhunting. Recently it has been a candidate for reintroduction into other parts of that cold land.

Surprisingly, there is a distinct difference of opinion on this plan. One school of thought resists every move to bring the musk ox back as a wild creature. Whether advocates of domestication will succeed in leading the shaggy beast into an orderly association with human communities remains to be seen. One thing is certain — they are dealing with one of the earth's most impressive examples of adaptation to environmental forces.

The musk ox has evolved in one of the harshest environments anywhere. It is a land of dwarf vegetation where winds of great force buffet the tundra, and winter temperatures commonly drop to 50 degrees below zero. Musk oxen once ranged the tundra all the way from Alaska to Greenland, according to Canadian biologist J. S. Tener, who has made perhaps the most detailed scientific study of this animal. Once there were even Siberian herds, but these are gone.

There are today, according to Tener's estimate, about 10,000 musk oxen in Canada, though only 1500 on the mainland. The rest are scattered across lonely and mostly uninhabited Arctic islands. Ellesmere Island alone has a musk-ox population estimated at 4000 animals. Wherever they survive in the wild, they are thinly scattered.

An adult musk ox is an impressive creature. Bulls are likely to weigh about 750 pounds, and the cows are somewhat smaller. They stand four to five feet at the shoulders. The sexes are colored alike; both have large shoulder humps. And both have horns that cap the skull and extend down beside the head, curling outward and upward.

Most impressive is the musk-ox fur, the "golden fleece" to those who hope to domesticate the animal. For survival, the musk ox needs one of the world's heaviest fur coats; the guard hairs are sometimes ten or twelve inches long.

The underwool of the musk ox is dense and soft, and said to be superior in quality to the finest cashmere. A mature animal sheds about five pounds of this shaggy "qiviut" each year. Hopefully, the domesticators expect the value of qiviut to become established at $35 to $50 a pound. They predict that a single animal might bring a return to an Eskimo herdsman of $200 a year. And the life expectancy of a musk ox is a quarter of a century.

On his natural range, where he subsists on willows and lichens, the musk ox — before the arrival of men — had little to fear except wolves, and perhaps now and then a barren ground grizzly. But by forming a defensive line or circle, with all the mature animals shoulder to shoulder facing outward, and the young with their sharp horns, behind and beneath the parents, musk oxen could make an attack difficult for wolves.

This defensive tactic, however, made the work of human hunters fairly simple — even with primitive weapons. And since musk oxen provided an excellent source of meat, early exploring parties as well as the crews of whaling ships decimated the creatures. One exploring party alone was said to have killed 600 musk oxen. It is not surprising that the animals were exterminated over much of their original range. Canada eventually passed a law protecting the musk oxen completely. But in Alaska it was already extinct.

In an effort to bring the musk ox back, the old U.S. Bureau of Biological Survey brought 34 animals from Greenland to Fairbanks, where they were held for five years of observation on the University

of Alaska's experimental farm at College. Then in 1935 and 1936 the 31 remaining animals were transferred to Nunivak National Wildlife Refuge and released.

On Nunivak Island, where there was no hunting, the animal the Eskimos called Oomingmak — "the bearded one" — prospered. Now, with musk oxen numbering about 800, the island is seriously overpopulated, a fact which causes concern among both federal and state biologists who would prefer that the Nunivak herd be half that large. Here, wildlife managers have a reservoir for reestablishing musk-ox herds on the Arctic Slope. But by 1968 only 23 had been released in the wild on the mainland — at a cost of $1200 per animal.

Musk oxen forming their wagon-train defense circle. *Hugh M. Halliday*

Meanwhile, at the University of Alaska's farm other musk oxen occupy rolling, lush-green brome-grass pastures behind tall and heavy wire fences. When I visited the farm, the herd — also started from twenty Nunivak calves captured by helicopter — numbered 44. The herdsman could see nothing ahead but prosperity and blue sky for the pioneering program. The animals had been relieved of those magnificent horns and stood in strange contrast to their wild relatives. The cows and calves were so docile and playful that photographing them was difficult because they stuck their noses against the lens. I never did trust the bulls.

Is this the musk ox of the future? There are those in positions of influence who disagree with the premise that there should be room in the North Country for both domestic and wild herds. Although Nunivak Island is a federal refuge, the musk oxen — as resident wildlife — belong to the state. And biologists from both state and federal agencies agree on the need to thin the refuge herd and rescue the range from overgrazing.

Consequently, the Alaska Board of Fish and Game advanced plans for a 1968 hunt in which 30 nonresidents would be granted permits at $1000 each. In this way the state hoped to accumulate funds to pay for transplanting musk oxen to portions of Alaska where they had been extirpated 100 years previously.

But opposition quickly arose. Musk-ox domesticators made their voices heard in the state capitol, and former Governor Walter J. Hickel promptly decreed there would be no season on the Nunivak musk oxen, although biologists insisted the Nunivak animals were endangering their range and health. The governor's announced reason was that he considered the shooting of musk oxen as unsporting. And some felt the governor had a point. It has been said that the shooting of a musk ox is a challenge equivalent to potting a Hereford steer.

But by digging a little deeper one finds why the others frowned on the $1000-a-permit hunt. The surplus animals, they say, might better be used to establish domestic herds. But more important, they do not want their intended domestic herds comingling with wild musk oxen. They fear the domestic animals will wander off with their free-roaming cousins, just as domesticated reindeer do today when the migrating caribou pass through their range in Arctic Alaska.

In truth, there has never been a thorough study of the carrying capacity of the slow-growing vegetation of the tundra where these animals would be expected to live. How far this domestic musk-ox program could go, how high its numbers, is not known. But at the university farm, musk-ox herdsman Larry Rubin insisted that Nunivak Island is far from overpopulated. The Alaska Conservation Society, which endorsed the thinning operation, quotes one opponent as saying Nunivak could support ten times as many musk oxen as it has. Wildlife biologists working on the refuge consider this most unlikely.

For the moment, the domesticators seem to have won. Their actions have stymied the hunt and have slowed efforts to transplant surplus musk oxen. But biologists worry about the possibility of a severe winter, with lengthy ice storms. Such winters occur with some frequency and might result in a musk-ox disaster due to starvation.

Unfortunately, as this and other developments reveal, the management of wildlife resources in Alaska has fallen into political hands. In the early years of statehood, the Fish and Game Department remained free to manage wildlife without weighing decisions in political terms. Alaska is widely considered to have one of the country's most capable staffs of professional wildlife workers. "For six years," a biologist in Juneau told me sadly, "our neophyte politicians didn't realize how much power they held. Now that they've discovered the political importance of fish and game, they are going to be difficult to deal with."

As a result of the swing toward politically oriented game management, biologists anticipate added emphasis on such discredited ideas as predator control and the introduction of exotics. One of the exotics currently popular there is the bison, not an Alaska native. Today herds of bison wander free not far from Fairbanks. And one state senator who is a bison fancier has requested a survey to determine where else in Alaska the buffalo might fit.

And for a classic example of political meddling in wildlife management, Alaskans can point to the now famous "Big Wolf Hunt," conducted in the Nelchina Basin in the 1967-68 winter.

Since long before the days of Red Riding Hood, wolves have been persecuted unreasonably. Across the Lower 48 they were eliminated in state after state. Alaska has its own hard core of citizens who would prefer to see their state completely free of wolves. Others are convinced the wolf is a valued and important member of Alaska's wildlife community.

A third group, the bounty hunters, do not want the wolves to disappear either — because they want enough left to chase in their sporty private aircraft.

Those who say that Alaska is so big, and the wolf so resourceful, that exterminating it in that sprawling state is impossible, will not find agreement from the state's foremost wolf expert, Robert A. Rausch. Rausch told me, "The most effective weapon of all against the wolf is the aircraft. If we don't restrict aircraft hunting, I predict that within ten years wolves will be in serious trouble all across the Arctic Slope. By permitting unrestricted use of aircraft, and continuing a high bounty, they could be wiped out in the Arctic within ten years. In the last fifteen years both pilots and aircraft have improved greatly." On the Kenai Peninsula wolves disappeared more than 60 years ago. Fortunately, a pack was spotted there during the winter of 1968-69.

Only poison ourpasses the aircraft as a wolf killer. What the plane can accomplish in the open country, poison could eventually do in the forests.

Across Alaska there is no universal opinion on how the state should treat its wolf population. Some, such as Fairbanks farmer Paul A. Elbert, loudly advocate the elimination of all wolves. In a letter printed in at least three Alaska publications, including the *Fairbanks*

News-Miner, Elbert wrote, "If I were a foreign agent paid to hurt Alaska all I could, I would cry 'preserve the wolf.' To me the campaign to preserve the wolves smacks of foreign sabotage and seems to fit right in with the demoralization of our youth, our judicial system, our financial structures, etc."

All the arguments were resurrected during 1967 when, sadly, wolves came out losers again, and the state's wolf management efforts slid back toward the Dark Ages. The argument began over a sprawling central Alaska region known as the Nelchina Basin, perhaps the state's most important outdoor recreation area.

For 20,000 square miles the Nelchina Basin, lying between Fairbanks and Anchorage, stretches from the Talkeetna River eastward to the Copper River, and from the Chugach Mountains to the Alaska Range. The herd of 80,000 caribou found within the basin yields from 3000 to 8000 a year to hunters. Here live more than 25,000 moose, many of them magnificent trophy bulls. There are also several thousand Dall sheep, plus both black and grizzly bears, all of which make the Nelchina important to a lot of Alaskans who hunt either for sport, or as many there still do, for meat.

When the U.S. Fish and Wildlife Service managed the wildlife resources of Alaska prior to statehood, the major effort on the Nelchina was toward killing predators, especially wolves. Between 1948 and 1954 government workers killed more than 200 wolves in the basin. Meanwhile, bounty hunters roamed the area and took an unknown number. By 1953 the wolf population for the entire basin was estimated at only twelve animals. Caribou and moose, on which the wolves prey, were increasing. Then in 1957, the Fish and Wildlife Service turned the Nelchina into a big study area and closed it to both wolf hunting and its own predator control activities. Following statehood, Alaska continued to keep the area closed. The

A caribou bull in summer. *Leonard Lee Rue III*

state was interested in maintaining and managing both the predator and prey species in their natural relationships. Following that low of 1953, the wolf population on the Nelchina increased gradually until it reached a peak of an estimated 400 to 450 in 1965.

Unfortunately for the wolves, the uncooperative caribou, due perhaps to a shortage of lichens, had begun a movement out of the Nelchina area. The harvest of caribou during the hunting season fell to about half of what it was the previous year, and hunters began looking around for something to blame. They did not have far to look.

In April 1965 the Alaska Senate jumped into the act. Accusing the Fish and Game Department of being dictatorial, high-handed, and arrogant, and the Board of Fish and Game of being a rubber stamp for the professionals, Senate Resolution No. 13 said that it "reaffirms its belief in the bounty system as the proper predator control for wolves; that under the law the wolf is a predator and not a trophy animal and the Department of Fish and Game is directed to discontinue any closed season for wolves and to end any area protection, that the Department is directed to pay wolf bounties forthwith."

Wildlife managers, however, knew the caribou herd was still at a high level. As the wolf population increased steadily, the caribou herd also underwent a steady buildup until it had almost doubled. But by 1965 wolf numbers in the Nelchina were already dropping drastically because many of the wolves had moved to adjoining regions with the caribou herds. Besides, in 1965, poachers were stepping up illegal wolf hunting in the Nelchina, especially the northern section of the basin. Rausch was even able to figure fairly closely the number of wolves shot unlawfully from airplanes that year. Field men found carcasses on the closed area. They interviewed suspected poachers and carefully analyzed their bounty records. At least 64 wolves had been poached in the closed area. But shortages of manpower and aircraft made law enforcement impossible.

And this Nelchina poaching angered law-abiding bounty hunters who knew that many of the wolves on which bounties were being paid by the state were coming from an area supposedly off-limits.

The pressure against keeping the Nelchina closed was felt acutely by the Alaska Board of Fish and Game, which ended up substituting the judgment of the legislature for that of its professional biologists. Not only did the board decree that there would be wolf hunting by permit on the Nelchina study area during the 1967–68 winter, but it also told the biologists how many wolves should be removed. For an authority they had the word of bounty hunters who assured them that the Nelchina Basin could safely yield up to 300 wolves.

To the wildlife biologists there was one big flaw in this advocated kill; they knew there were no longer 300 wolves in the Nelchina Basin. In two separate wolf counts on the area in the fall of 1967, they had learned that the Nelchina held a maximum of 200 wolves. Rausch urged that the kill be held to 75 wolves. Consequently, in a news release early in February 1968, the Department of Fish and Game limited the kill to 75 to be taken on three weekend hunts with 25 permits issued for each weekend.

A week later, spurred on by wolf hunters and wolf haters, the policy-setting Board of Fish and Game descended on Juneau, to do battle with its staff. Accusing the professionals of purposely misinterpreting its order, the angry board announced that it would tell them how many wolves to take from the Nelchina. The board insisted that the area be opened seven days a week, October 1st to March 31st, until 300 dead wolves had come out of the basin. It was, in effect, an order to exterminate the wolf population across 20,000 square miles of Alaska.

The new regulation also opened most of the rest of Alaska to wolf hunting with no limit and no closed season. One exception was the Kenai, where the season remained closed. "Hell, there haven't been any wolves on that area for 60 years anyhow," I was told by one state worker.

In other parts of Alaska the wolf has also suffered. This is especially true in the Petersburg-Wrangell area where the Sitka deer, a small subspecies of the Columbia blacktail, is common food on the family table. There are an estimated quarter-million Sitka deer in southeastern Alaska. Hunters take only about 12,000 annually, and have an annual bag limit of four deer.

In the last couple of years, however, hunters have noticed that their four-deer limit is harder to come by. There must be a reason. Wolves? "He's always a handy scapegoat," said Celia M. Hunter, executive secretary of the Alaska Conservation Society, recounting the sequence of events. With the wolf population apparently healthy, and deer numbers down, local residents convinced their state legislators that it was time to deal the wolf a blow — either that or watch him take the deer that rightfully belonged to people. Unfortunately, there was no scientific evidence to indicate they were either right or wrong.

Caught in the middle was longtime career wildlife biologist Pete Nelson, who had lived in Alaska since 1948, working for the U.S. Fish and Wildlife Service. He had retired in Juneau and then become Commissioner of the Department of Fish and Game. He told me, "One of the first tasks I had after I came on the job was to review the budget. In it there was an item of $15,000 for wolf control." It had been written in not by the Board of Fish and Game, but by a legislative subcommittee unhampered by biological facts. "I was told," Nelson recalled, "that's not law. It's worse than law. If I chose to ignore it, the next time the legislature could cut out of the budget everything we really wanted.

"They were attributing to the wolves," Nelson explained, "what was due to slightly diminished hunting pressure contributing to an overpopulation of deer, which put the range in bad shape." Although he attempted to explain that "the wolf is doing a pretty good job of deer control," the legislators had ordered poison.

Finally Nelson stated his belief that, "If you must use poison, use 1080." That succinct statement stirred up a storm of protest far beyond the state's boundaries. The poison 1080 is in ill-repute everywhere, except perhaps among some of the federal government's professional predator control agents.

But Nelson, protesting the use of any poison, said he would have nothing to do with strychnine — which was the poison eventually used — "because it kills eagles and everything else." Nelson says it was this issue which led to his replacement as commissioner by Augie Reetz, a political appointee chosen by then Governor Hickel.

Far to the north where the federal government's Bureau of Indian Affairs is still hand-feeding a faltering 50-year-old domestic reindeer project, the wolf also remains under constant threat at taxpayers' expense. The aim is economic aid for the Seward Peninsula Eskimos by converting them to herdsmen and butchers. Whether reindeer will meet the need still remains to be seen. The problems are numerous and complex, and the wolf is perhaps one of the lesser hazards. The reindeer have a built-in potential for overgrazing the range and roaming away with wild caribou. Marketing problems are still unsolved. The plan is to lend an Eskimo herder a starter herd from a government "model herd" maintained at Nome which, after five years, is to be repaid in kind.

Understandably, wolves do prey on the reindeer. The Fish and Wildlife Service, fulfilling an agreement with its sister agency, the Bureau of Indian Affairs, controls these Seward Peninsula wolves by strychnine, airplane hunting, and occasionally by the use of "coyote-getters" (or cyanide guns) in remote areas. The plane and pilot used for this wolf control work are maintained at Kotzebue. In five years the Fish and Wildlife wolf-chasers have removed 58 wolves from the vicinity of the reindeer herds, while utilizing the plane to help herders round up their reindeer, supposedly scattered by marauding wolves.

So the long-persecuted wolf, reduced to one last stronghold, was under attack on one front after the other. The controversy over the big wolf hunt on the Nelchina — which took at least 115 wolves in its first year — demonstrated that wolves do have friends. A growing number of Alaskans say that there is room for the wolf in their state, that the big carnivore has a special role in the interrelationships of the wildlife community.

The 1968 Alaska Legislature passed two laws related to the wolf bounty question. One calls for approval from the Board of Fish and Game for the spreading of poisons. The other handed the board authority for establishing bounty areas, enabling it to do away with bounties where it might so choose.

But the powerful antiwolf faction also seems to have its major den in the legislature. Unwilling to permit the professional biologists to counsel them, the legislators had taken steps to force the Alaska Department of Fish and Game deeper than ever into the predator control business. In fact, faced with decreasing federal interest in predator control, the state, on occasion, appeared to be developing its own branch of predator control. In April 1968, Alaska's commissioners listened to Homer Ford, the U.S. Fish and Wildlife Service supervisor of the northwestern region, present an orientation program on 1080 and other materials for coyote control in western states. This interest in killing predators has its counterpart in the early development of state after state across the West. People conditioned to the widespread use of predator control methods perpetuate the myth that killing off all the predators guarantees a brighter tomorrow. So Alaska could well wipe out its wolves. "It will be a sad country," says Rausch, "when there is no longer room for an occasional wolf or wolverine."

Obviously, Alaska's wolves deserve a better break. What Rausch and many others, including the Alaska Conservation Society, would like to see is the elevation of the wolf to its rightful place in the roster of big game trophy animals. Those who might oppose this on the grounds that the wolf deserves full protection at all times should face the fact that as long as wolf populations are fairly high, there are not three but two alternatives. Either the wolf becomes a legitimate trophy or it retains its current status as a predator. Predators, and especially wolves, are also subject to the selfish interests of a minority group of private aircraft owners seeking games to play.

One justification sometimes mentioned in support of the long discredited bounty system is that bounties serve as welfare measures. Supposedly, impoverished Eskimos and Indians can hunt bountied animals and live on the proceeds. But a majority of those who would hunt wolves for bounty are seldom impoverished. If they were, they would neither own costly aircraft nor have the money to keep them in fuel. Hunting wolves is the way they get their kicks. The bounty which the state pays them for each wolf so taken, plus the sale of the pelt which may bring another $75 to $100, helps cover the cost of their hobby.

The wolf is chased out into the open where his tracks show plainly in the fresh snow. He has no place to hide and no prospect of survival. There is no stalking, no matching of wits, only a powerful, roaring airplane pursuing a wild dog until he can no longer run. The wolf may as well give up, and quite often does, simply stopping in his tracks and waiting for death. He is shot from the air. One pilot and his assistant in a recent year "turned in" 82 wolves for bounty. The only risk facing the pilot on this strafing mission is the possibility of running his plane into the ground.

In 1968, with the Nelchina fiasco fresh in mind, State Senator Lowell Thomas, Jr., of Anchorage introduced a bill to abolish bounty payments on wolves, wolverines, and coyotes. It failed to muster the needed votes. Eventually, Commissioner Augie Reetz announced that wolf bounties would be paid over most of the state. He made one exception, the Nelchina Basin.

Even experienced bounty hunters sometimes "stray" across boundaries of Mount McKinley National Park, where all wildlife is protected. Wildlife biologist Wayne P. Merry, who works on the park staff, reported that two such hunters, "both with many, many wolf hunting hours in this area," were caught inside the park and claimed that they didn't know where the park boundaries were.

And in the years prior to Senator Thomas' proposal, the state paid out more than $211,000 of tax money on bounties. Happily, Alaska has since reduced the area where wolf bounties are in effect.

But in the long run — and it may not take so long at the rate the developers are now descending — the big threat to Alaska's wildlife promises to come through changes inflicted on the landscape. Great fields of coal lie within strip-mining depth of the surface. An anticipated price increase in gold will put the dredges back to work, turning over the earth and muddying the streams. Oil crews have descended on the estuaries and the coastal wilderness, bringing roads, machinery, people, and villages.

Even wildlife refuges stand to be invaded increasingly by industrial forces eager to extract oil as well as hard-rock minerals. The great Arctic National Wildlife Range lies but a short distance east of the mammoth oil strike on Prudhoe Bay. Former Governor Walter J. Hickel of Alaska had asked then Secretary of the Interior Stewart L. Udall to permit oil exploration crews to enter the refuge. The secretary turned down this request because of the threat promised to the unique resources of the area.

To the extent that the landscape of Alaska is threatened by the impending all-out rush for economic development in the North, the wildlife living there is likely to be viewed as decreasingly important.

Conservationists agree that if Alaska is to keep its abundance and variety of wild creatures, plans for conserving the wildlife resources must be included in the planning for the state's development. Otherwise the future of the wolves, wolverines, big game animals, waterfowl, eagles, salmon, and other wild creatures stands in the shadow of a giant question mark.

5

The Beautiful Sad Face
of Amchitka

ON AMCHITKA ISLAND, famous stronghold of the once endangered sea
otter, bustling crews of technicians and heavy-equipment operators
repeatedly prepare for the most earthshaking parties ever staged
within a national wildlife refuge. And the sea otters swimming in
the shallow waters there face their most recent threat — the atom
bomb.

To get a firsthand look at what is happening today on this island,
I arrived in Anchorage prepared to travel out into the Aleutian
Islands. For several weeks I had corresponded with officials of the
Atomic Energy Commission, seeking permission to visit this part
of the Aleutian Islands National Wildlife Refuge. I found that I
was a rarity. Journalists flock to world-famed fun cities, with their
incessant syncopated beat, but rarely does one ask to go to
Amchitka — lonely, windswept, fog-bound.

Going there is not easy. Despite the fact that this has been a
national wildlife refuge since 1913, the Atomic Energy Commission
has the final word these days on who may or may not go to Amchitka.

The commercial airline connecting the island with Anchorage on
twice-weekly flights is forbidden to sell Amchitka tickets to passen-

gers without prior approval from the AEC. The rule holds as firmly for U.S. Fish and Wildlife Service personnel, including the refuge manager, as it does for visiting writers. There are no facilities on Amchitka except those maintained for contract workers. But once the Atomic Energy Commission, in 1968, permitted me to witness activities on this refuge island, they were both courteous and helpful. I had complete freedom to go where I liked and photograph what I cared to. The operation's top-secret phase had not yet begun.

Through the morning our plane droned across the North Pacific toward Asia and the Orient. Below us somewhere, hidden by a thick layer of marshmallow clouds, lay the Alaska Peninsula and beyond it the Aleutians, that great curved chain of islands which long ago fired the imagination of explorers and naturalists.

Toward the end of the morning we nosed through the cloud bank and touched down in a misty rain on a 9000-foot paved runway, a legacy from World War II when Amchitka was an air force base. Inside the little white terminal building there was a sign on the wall — "Amchitka Island Is Part of the Aleutian Islands National Wildlife Refuge." Amchitka resembled no other wildlife refuge I had seen.

About 70 people had alighted from the plane and they now milled about waiting for their luggage. Outside the terminal, construction company vehicles were arriving and departing. Across the way workmen crawled over a huge hangar, one of two being restored after the years of abandonment since World War II. Long lines of supplies flanked the runway and waited on paved areas for removal to other parts of the island. In the days that followed I was to get a closer look at this incredible activity underway on Amchitka.

What the visitor to Amchitka sees depends on his background, his interests, and his mission. The engineer coming to this lonely island in the North Pacific might be filled with a sense of pride in the shadow of the world's most powerful well-drilling equipment. The military historian could stand on the tundra, gazing out across the island with a faraway glint in his eyes of another time when the world belonged to the soldier. The landscape painter might find inspiration in the lonely rockbound beaches with their great black rocks standing boldly against the pounding of giant breakers and rising surf. But the ecologist or naturalist, thinking back to a time before men touched this wild American treasure island with their black magic, finds himself overcome with a deep sadness. He feels a revulsion, as an artist would standing before an ancient masterpiece defiled by vandals.

The Aleutians are the home of the sea otter, Steller's sea lion, bald eagle, gray-crowned rosy finches, the nearly extinct little Aleutian Canada goose, and a host of other wild creatures. Where it has not yet been defiled, the Aleutian chain is an island realm of rare beauty and verdant vegetation of sea grasses and brilliant wildflowers. The Aleutians, cradle of violent storms and home of earthquakes, possess in their wild and primitive beauty a character of their own. They are a national treasure as surely as the Everglades or the Canyonlands. But their sheer remoteness has kept them out of the public eye.

From the end of the Alaska Peninsula southwestward there are some 200 islands, 70 of them large enough and important enough to have been named. For 1100 miles the "chain" reaches in a great sweeping arc of steppingstones separating the Bering Sea from the North Pacific. They are grouped into little families of islands with the Near Islands, which include Attu, being the farthest from the American mainland. The next major group to the east is the Rat Islands, of which Amchitka is best known.

The Pacific beach of Amchitka Island. *Alaska Pictorial Service*

Amchitka, lying as far south as London, has ice-free harbors the year round. It is 42 miles long, $4\frac{1}{2}$ miles wide at its broadest point, and has an area of 114 square miles. Its irregular shores slope gently to the ocean's edge in some places and in others fall away in sheer rock cliffs. Storms drive ashore great white-capped breakers that sometimes force the sea otters to take refuge in the quieter waters of secluded bays. On the rocky crags, eagles nest. In the shallows all around the island, kelp grows in profusion, sending its long brown strands out to lie on the surface pointing in the direction of the tidal flow.

The eastern part of Amchitka, where the human activity is concentrated, is low land rising no higher than 351 feet above sea level. Toward its middle part the island rises to gently rolling terrain and tableland. And toward the northwestern end, mountains reach to 1335 feet. There are a few streams and, especially in the central section, numerous shallow ponds and lakes. Some of these waters harbor a native population of Dolly Varden trout and serve as salmon nurseries.

Mosses and lichens flourish and there are brilliant dwarf wildflowers. The spongy tundra is dotted with three species of dwarf willow, the island's only native trees. "This is *Salix arctica*, the tallest native tree on the island," a U.S. Fish and Wildlife Service refuge biologist told me one day, as he bent down to examine a wind-stunted willow scarcely two inches high,

People who have come here have often come less from choice than necessity. Soldiers stationed on these remote wilderness lands during World War II cursed the Aleutians. They despised the climate and loneliness. Amchitka has some of the world's worst weather. It is said jokingly here that one should be thankful for those days when he can see the toes of his boots because he can be sure there is at least a six-foot ceiling. For 60 percent of the year the cloud ceilings are below 1000 feet and visibility is less than three miles. But this is not a particularly cold region. The lowest recorded temperature is 15 degrees, but on any summer day winds blowing off the ocean may make warm jackets welcome.

At least twenty pairs of bald eagles nest on the island. Great sea lions, perhaps 400, haul out to rest on the rocky ledges at the bases of the storm-washed cliffs. Seals bob among the sea otters in the kelp beds. In the nesting season puffins, cormorants, murres, and guillemots come in from the ocean to nest in crowded colonies among the glaucous-winged gulls. Sea ducks pass back and forth in tight flying formation. There arc no large mammals on the island, only the Norway rats that came with the troops during World War II, jumped ship, and established themselves.

Best known of the island's wildlife are the sea otters that occupy the bays around Amchitka. This adroit water-loving mammal is a favorite with nearly everyone coming to Amchitka — one of the few things that many have found interesting enough to write home about.

Following the discovery of the Aleutians in 1741 by Vitus Bering, there came the free-lance fur gatherers. These *promyshlenniki* became thc scourge of the islands. In a parade of pillage that was to last as long as the otter supply held, they pressed thc Aleuts into slavery, forcing them to seek out the sea otters from their small boats and kill them. Disease, murder, and slavery reduced to perhaps 3000 the estimated 20,000 Aleuts originally living in the islands.

Amchitka's abuse began long ago. In 1921, according to refuge records, native residents at Atka brought to Amchitka seven blue foxes and released them to fend for themselves, live off the land, multiply, and become the basis for an annual fur harvest. The federal government had granted them a permit for this transfer of alien

An Arctic blue fox and thick-billed murres. Sea birds were decimated by these introduced foxes, now eliminated from Amchitka. *Karl W. Kenyon*

foxes. Sadly, it is also noted that when these first foxes arrived, Amchitka was populated with the Aleutian Canada geese, now vanished from that island.

By 1925, the fox harvest had begun with a take of 172 pelts. The total trapped there by the end of the next decade was 4076 with a listed value of $183,360. By 1936, with fox furs falling in value and that industry in a bad way, trapping ceased. The foxes increased and continued to live off the native wildlife. Except for howling winds and crashing surf, Amchitka became quiet. It was a wild place where men seldom ventured — a lonely American wilderness. Even the two small buildings erected by the old Bureau of Fisheries for its otter wardens would soon disappear. But the island was not destined to remain uninhabited. During World War II, thousands of troops were stationed here.

I had heard that the litter of war was still scattered across Amchitka's tundra, but without seeing it, one can scarcely visualize the extent of this subarctic junkyard. The standard dwelling of World War II soldiers in remote areas was the Quonset hut, a semicircular steel dungeon resting on a wooden platform. The island once held perhaps 3200 such buildings. Despite two abortive salvage efforts, the majority of the Quonsets are still there, half fallen, partly decayed, and interspersed with wooden walkways, gun emplacements, rows of telephone poles, old mess halls, shops, and even a stockade. This is the scene I remember — green tundra cut by vehicle tracks still showing after a quarter of a century, serving as a background for a great ghost town of gray Quonset huts, still standing a generation after their abandonment.

The southeastern third of the island is a junkyard. But along the roads one comes occasionally to the real dumps. Wrecked planes, thousands of oil drums, and assorted other refuse have been piled out of the way in a few chosen spots. A century from now it may still be there, somewhat weathered but much in evidence. One can scarcely argue with the use of the island in a time of world war when enemy troops were on American soil only a few islands away. But clearing away the debris of war would seem a legitimate cost of the conflict to a country that has spent untold millions to help other nations recover from the same war. In the Aleutians, however, wartime junk is out of sight, hence out of mind.

After World War II the uninhabited island was left once more

More than 3000 quonsets were left to decay on
Amchitka after World War II. *Karl W. Kenyon*

to the eagles, the remnant populations of sea otters, and the rats that had jumped ship. But as early as 1950 someone was again interested in using Amchitka. That spring a plane arrived on the island's airstrip loaded with investigators who went about their inspection in secrecy and brushed aside questions concerning their intrusion into a national wildlife refuge. Even then their plan was to explode an underground bomb. But the island was found to be somehow unsuitable, and they folded their blueprints, boarded their ships, and departed. The visit, however, had cast a foreboding shadow over Amchitka.

Years were to pass before the shadow gained substance. Statehood came for Alaska and with it the authority over the sea otters went from the federal to the state government. This brought state biologists into the picture, and since then the Alaskans have cooperated closely with federal refuge personnel, carrying out their sea otter management using the federal lands as a base. This was the orderly, unhurried state of affairs on Amchitka early in the 1960's when the Department of Defense began moving in.

There is evidence that the Department of Defense was at first making its own decisions without letting even the President in on its thinking. Pierre Salinger, press secretary to President Kennedy, makes passing mention of the subject in his book *With Kennedy*. Defense Department Press Secretary Arthur Sylvester once reported to Salinger that plans were then in motion to carry out atomic testing in Alaska. Salinger, sensing the implications of such testing so near the Soviet border, took the matter to the President. It was news to the Chief Executive. The President called Secretary of Defense Robert McNamara. But the Defense Department had not even informed its Secretary of the atomic testing plans for the Aleutians. As Salinger recalls, the whole idea came to a "shattering stop."

Obviously, the Department of Defense succeeded in setting its plans in motion once more. In 1963 President Johnson assumed office. In 1964 the Department of Defense began active preparations for an atomic explosion on Amchitka. The Department of Defense and the Governor of Alaska made a joint announcement about the impending atomic underground blast, called "Long Shot."

From this point forward the concern of conservationists was twofold. They were worried about the safety of the sea otters; there was no experience to tell anyone what the explosion might do to the animals. They were also concerned about the added destruction the Department of Defense might bring to this island and whether or not they would "police up" their operation as they had promised.

As anyone visiting Amchitka today can see, they did not follow through on this promise. The site of the 1965 Long Shot is obviously a place the military considered unworthy of being left as they found it. The roofed frame of a steel building still stands there, and littering the surrounding countryside is a collection of remnant metal and wooden waste materials left where they fell.

At the time, those in charge of Long Shot also promised concerned conservationists that their plans called for only a single nuclear blast on Amchitka. This was quickly brought to AEC's attention when that agency began moving in on the island later for a series of four tests, and I have talked with several persons present at the meeting at which Defense Department officials made the "one shot" promise. But the Atomic Energy Commission points out that *it* cannot be held responsible for Department of Defense statements. Adding that the AEC never made any such promise, that agency's officials draw the line hard and fast between itself and Defense, which first invaded the same island for similar purposes.

The Long Shot operation in 1965 was designed to test our country's ability to detect underground nuclear blasts in Russia. Now Amchitka has become a full-fledged test site itself. And no one can say for certain when or if the AEC will leave.

In preparation for these new tests, specialists from the Las Vegas headquarters of AEC investigated at least one other possible Alaska site. This was near Point Lay on the Arctic Ocean, and not in a national wildlife refuge. Barge shipments there, however, would have to be limited to ice-free months, and there already was a landing strip on Amchitka. There may have been other reasons influencing the choice. Some Alaskans have advanced the idea that the oil industry frowned on the Atomic Energy Commission exploding underground nuclear devices in the Arctic where there is feverish oil exploration. "They didn't want us in their oil patches," one contract worker on the Amchitka site told me.

Why not confine these latest tests to the deserts of Nevada, where other AEC explosions have been set off? Public Affairs Director Henry G. Vermillion of the AEC Las Vegas installation explained frankly that the planned tests were too powerful for Nevada. The biggest one detonated there to date was a megaton and it rattled windows in Las Vegas and brought unhappy reactions from the public. "What we needed," said Vermillion, "was distance from population centers and the right geologic conditions."

As nearly as biologists could learn, the wildlife around Amchitka and nearby islands suffered little damage from Long Shot itself. Whether or not the coming tests will have as little damaging effect on the wildlife as the AEC hopes remains to be seen. The planned explosions would, as one Alaskan expressed it, "make Long Shot look like a firecracker."

The question frequently comes up as to whether or not Long Shot did vent and permit radiation seepage from the hole. Presumably it did, even though geologists had calculated that no leakage of radioactive products into the surrounding sea would appear for a period of 400 years. Minute amounts have been found in the water near the site in the last two or three years, but it measures out, I am told, as insufficient (by Federal Radiation Council standards) to cause any concern.

Yet this raises the specter of substantial leakage from the forthcoming, far more powerful blasts, and the question of possible biological harm to the food chains of the North Pacific and our Pacific Coast fisheries, since the Japan Current flows from west to east.

But there are forms of damage aside from those resulting from the blast itself. The presence of people brings its own kind of damage. The atomic tests have altered Fish and Wildlife Service plans for this portion of the refuge. One phase of the plan began with a Herculean campaign to eliminate the imported foxes. By the time the foxes were finally wiped out in 1962, the island's birdlife was rebounding with amazing vigor. Ducks had increased in numbers, and the loons, always vulnerable to the predation of the foxes, were returning. Other birds, forced to nest on cliff faces and offshore islets, began to spread once more and to occupy the island. Amchitka was again fulfilling its historic role as an island bird refuge of major importance.

Then came Long Shot. Bird populations apparently suffered from the presence of large numbers of people. The later arrival of AEC contractors continued the pressure, and nesting bird populations are suffering a downhill trend. Basic in the aims of those working to eradicate the foxes from Amchitka was the plan to bring the Aleutian Canada goose back to this portion of its original range. According to the plan, the progeny of captive populations were to be returned to Amchitka. The detonation of Long Shot put an abrupt halt to that restoration project. Today, with still more bombs in the offing, the biologists who understand the wildlife picture along the Aleutians have decided that risking the geese on Amchitka would not be a sound expenditure. These are secretive birds requiring far less disturbance than they would encounter on Amchitka today. Instead, another island, Agattu, has been readied for the initial restocking of the geese if the birds do not return there of their own accord.

But Agattu lives beneath its own shadow. The U.S. Air Force until recently was studying it for some mysterious top-secret use. The near invasion of Agattu by the Defense Department was strongly protested by the National Audubon Society. But presumably any branch of the defense establishment might turn its attention again to this wild and beautiful outpost, where foxes have been all but eliminated and the birds have returned in force as they had once come back to Amchitka. On Agattu, barring some new human invasion, this endangered little goose may take its first step back from oblivion's edge.

Despite its invasion of a national wildlife refuge, the Atomic Energy Commission seeks to be counted among the "good guys." It has concern for its public image. It makes serious efforts to carry out its Amchitka mission with as little damage as possible to the environment. Unfortunately for the AEC, it inherited, with Amchitka, one of the greatest concentrations of sea otters anywhere. This little fur-covered hot potato has brought widespread attention to the Amchitka activities of the AEC.

Biologists with the Alaska Department of Fish and Game had, for some time, been developing plans to remove surplus sea otters from Amchitka to other areas where the native populations had been extirpated. If the AEC, the Alaskans reasoned, were introducing a threat of unknown proportions to the Alaskan sea otter population, that agency should aid the state in its plans to hasten the transplanting of surplus animals from Amchitka.

As a result, the Alaska Department of Fish and Game, the AEC, and the U.S. Bureau of Sport Fisheries and Wildlife all cooperated during the summer of 1969 in the most massive otter moving project ever undertaken. During the weeks of otter netting and transplanting, 359 animals, perhaps ten percent of the Amchitka otter population, were caught and moved to new locations. This was paid for by the AEC, which had allotted nearly $200,000 for the project.

Until recently, at least, no one knew how much shock a sea otter could survive. The Battelle Memorial Institute of Columbus, Ohio, a leading independent research agency, is the AEC contractor in charge of biological research on the Amchitka site. The question of the sea otter's shock threshold was handed to Battelle, which designed special equipment to measure this unknown.

The laboratory device sat in a dark corner of a big hangar building when I was on the island. It is a cylindrical tank welded of extremely heavy-gauge steel, equipped with a heavy screw-down steel lid. The tank, painted barn red and wearing a small tag declaring it the property of the United States Government, is perhaps eight feet long and five feet in diameter.

The testing method was simple. Saltwater was pumped into the tank, then a sea otter was dropped in. The lid was sealed. Next, a 20-mm cannon was exploded in such a manner that a piston was depressed and the pressure per square inch could be measured mathematically. Finally the tank was opened and the otter removed to see what the explosion had done to him.

Early in the summer of 1968, Battelle workers completed their tests with this tank and concluded, after killing twelve otters in the chamber, that sea otters die if exposed to about 300 pounds per square inch. I did not learn whether or not there was any measurement of harmful sublethal effects. Nor did I learn whether the experimenters computed a stress factor to correct for the shock an otter might suffer when caught and imprisoned in a totally dark tank prior to firing the cannon.

Aside from the threat to the sea otters and other wildlife around Amchitka, conservationists are justifiably concerned about the surface damage being done to the island. Here again the Atomic Energy Commission makes conscientious efforts to hold down its damage. But it is virtually impossible to conduct such concentrated activity on Amchitka without damaging that fragile landscape.

Tundra carries the scars of abuse for decades. One day we flew at low altitudes over Amchitka. Below us were networks of military vehicle tracks still boldly evident after a quarter of a century. The contractors working for the AEC have been ordered to keep their vehicles on the designated roads and to take other precautionary measures to keep from damaging the area further. But where new roads are needed, new roads are built. One contract let by the AEC was for converting 20 miles of a primitive vehicle trail left from World War II into an all-weather, two-lane road up the center of the island. A spur road was built by heavy equipment pushing the tundra aside, then pushing the subsoil out on both sides of the road for distances of an estimated 75 or 100 feet, thus leaving a row of spoil banks much more extensive than necessary.

There were 480 men on Amchitka in the summer of 1968. There was also a plan for new living areas sufficient to bring the island's population up to nearly 1000 men. Mobile homes have been shipped in and set up to form camps. Supporting this bustling community was a fleet of 255 vehicles ranging from pickup trucks to mammoth tractor-trailer rigs.

Amchitka now has its own post office with its own zip code. There is a well-staffed medical center equipped with the necessary ambulances, a fire station with the latest in fire-fighting equipment, an Alaska state patrolman whose salary is paid by the AEC, a small library, theater, and liquor store, all operated by contractors and subcontractors.

The old boat dock has been renovated and rendered serviceable for receiving bargeloads of heavy supplies. One boat tied up at the Amchitka dock during my visit was delivering long sections of 54-inch steel casings shipped up from Louisiana to line the drill holes. A towering derrick lifted the casings from the barge one at a time and set them onto a huge truck, which lumbered off across the island to store them in long rows until needed. The airstrip has been equipped with radar, ground control, and a lighting system to make it what one official called "the most modern civilian airfield in Alaska." The Amchitka operation was reported to be costing $58 million that year alone.

All of this is to speed up the drilling of some of the biggest and straightest holes men have ever sunk into the heart of the earth. At present the AEC plans a four-shot series of blasts in the depths of these holes. To prevent the leakage of radioactive materials into the atmosphere, each of these explosions must occur more than a mile beneath the surface. One afternoon I visited the site of one of these drilling operations, where the crew was sinking a hole of 90-inch diameter to a depth of 6200 feet. The 3000-horsepower drilling rig can lift two million pounds. It was, I was told, the world's most powerful drilling equipment. After one of these holes has been extended to its specified depth, it is fitted with a steel casing held in place by a wall of concrete. Workmen were to be lowered with mine-shaft elevators to the base of the hole. There they would

A giant drilling rig and its refuse near the shore of Amchitka,
now the site of underground nuclear blasts. *George Laycock*

excavate a room 31 feet in diameter and 61 feet high to be walled
with steel and with plastic concrete to receive the "device." The
biggest hole planned for this series was to be 120 inches — 10
feet — in diameter.

The expert drillers operating this equipment are old hands from
the oil patches of Texas and Oklahoma. A crew of twenty men keeps

one of these drills going 24 hours a day. It takes them about a year to drill the hole.

To remove the drillings from the hole, the workmen feed in and pump out "mud." This material is bentonite, which is commonly used to seal ponds against water leakage. The "mud," shipped to Amchitka in huge collapsible rubber containers, costs about $5 a barrel. During each minute of drilling, 4000 gallons of bentonite flows across the cutting edge to pick up the solids. What happens to the "mud" as it comes from the drill hole? It is pumped into large settling lagoons. Then, tall draglines scoop out the settlings and move this material aside for burial in nearby pits.

At first, instead of digging pits down to a solid base, the contractors simply chose to form settling ponds by scooping up dikes. Because of the nature of the soil and the nature of the "mud" being circulated through the holes, these dikes would not retain the materials. The soils of the Aleutians are relatively young, and they lack those cohesive qualities which would enable them to compact and form a barrier for the mixture used in the drilling. Consequently, the materials seep through the dikes and through the tundra beneath them, sometimes polluting trout streams, natural salmon nursery ponds, and even flowing into the bays at the mouth of streams.

One of the major streams on Amchitka is Rifle Range Creek. Contract fisheries investigators, using shockers on the stream in 1967, checked and released 167 fish. Less than a year later they could find only fourteen fish. A film of oil sometimes covered the water.

Earthmoving equipment is changing the face of Amchitka in more ways than one. There is a borrow pit along Rifle Range Road. Begun in World War II, it became known as the Galleon Pit. The AEC contractors have greatly enlarged it, and now it is a scar covering the slope of a hill reminiscent of a strip-mine operation. Recently, however, they moved this borrow pit operation across the road and opened a new pit. I was told that it would be too costly to keep on taking materials from the old pit they had started.

Pollution from the settling ponds could have been reduced by greater care on the part of the contractors. For example, one day a drilling crew was making good speed with its work at a site above a small, deep-running creek. The "mud" pumped out of the hole filled the settling pond. At this point the drilling should have been stopped until there was storage space for the mud. But instead the work went on and the lagoon overflowed.

The pollutant, which has an oil content of about four percent, flowed into the creek and toward the Bering Sea. It turned the creek from clear water to a milky color. As well as sealing holes in the earth, the mud will close the pores of plants and clog the gills of fish. In this instance it had flowed into waters which supported a population of Dolly Varden trout. Observers on the banks of the creek watched the pollutant discolor the creek. Then they saw the first trout swimming erratically upstream on its back, scooting from side to side and seemingly trying to leap out of the water. There was oil in the water on that day, but the chances are that the fish were dying from suffocation as the "mud" sealed their gills and shut off their oxygen.

There can be little doubt that officials high up in the Atomic Energy Commission are sincere about their desires to protect this island against such damage as they can and still stay there. But one difficulty comes from having their instructions carried out at various levels through contractors, subcontractors, and machinery operators. The AEC has reached agreements with the U.S. Fish and Wildlife Service aimed at protecting this terrain wherever possible. The Fish and Wildlife Service asked the AEC during the early days of its

Amchitka project to stand the cost of two refuge managers and two biologists, to form rotating two-man teams which would be present on the island at all times. To cover the cost of the two managers, the AEC allocated $50,000. The biologists were provided a year later when the AEC added another $60,000 to its investment to cover their salaries and expenses. The biologists' duties include close observation of wildlife on and around the island through the time of the blasts, and they are to study any resultant damage. The two refuge management agents, meanwhile, are kept busy during their rotation of island duty watch-dogging the contractors.

Because of the wording of the original 1913 executive order establishing the Aleutian Islands National Wildlife Refuge, agencies dealing with defense work feel free to come on this refuge whenever they choose. President William Howard Taft had included in that order the statement, "The establishment of this reservation shall not interfere with the use of the islands for lighthouse, military, or naval purposes . . . " Whether it had been his intention that this wording automatically justifies use of the refuge for weapons testing in peacetime should, perhaps, be reviewed.

How long will the AEC be using Amchitka for testing its "devices"? No one seems to have any firm thoughts on the question. The current program was planned for five years, I was told, and already one and a half years had passed.

It was impressed upon me that AEC's plans are malleable. If it should develop that Amchitka does not measure up geologically, the work will be moved to a new site. Where that might be is anyone's guess, but Point Lay would likely get first consideration. Officials insist that there is no plan to operate test facilities in both areas. Apparently Point Lay would come back into the picture only if Amchitka were a washout for some scientific reason. Then, if Point

Lay proved unsatisfactory, the AEC would look at other lands, and the national wildlife refuge system could again be endangered.

In its search for stemming materials to pack the drill holes after the atomic devices are in place, the AEC turned its attention to the neighboring island of Adak. It later found a source of such materials on Amchitka. The AEC then began casting about for suitable sites for outposts on other islands from which it might telemeter the

proposed shots, before settling on already war-wracked Kiska.

Likewise, the Atomic Energy Commission was constructing an unmanned weather station with a single tower on Kiska, the data to be telemetered to Amchitka. The agency has apparently dropped another plan to install a similar station on the wild little island of Semisopochnoi.

Obviously, the AEC will move onto other lands within the refuge

Amchitka Island — a Steller sea lion rookery. *Alaska Pictorial Service*

as it sees fit. And whatever steps it takes are likely to be taken quietly at first. Conservationists within the Alaska Conservation Society noted that the details of the AEC plan to move onto Amchitka were kept quiet and even denied until the governor of Alaska and the AEC issued their joint announcement. Nor had any word come out of the Fish and Wildlife Service, which although aware of the plans, had top-level orders to cooperate. As a result, the plans were already completed and approved before conservationists could learn enough about the nuclear testing project to muster any objections.

As I left Amchitka, rain was falling, clouds were hanging close to the rocky shores, and fog softened the harsh outlines of the man-made structures. I looked out across the hills and tablelands as far as the fog would permit, hoping for a last glimpse of that wild, unique stronghold of the sea otter and the bald eagle. But wherever I looked there were the old Quonset huts, vehicle tracks, and the bustling centers of present activity — all overshadowed by the tall drilling rigs on the horizon.

I had seen the sad face of Amchitka.

Moving Day
for Sea Otters

THE PROMISE OF ADVENTURE had awakened me early. At dawn I dressed in heavy clothing against buffeting winds coming off the Bering Sea. Then I pulled on a rubber suit against the fog and the rain that would probably come before we returned.

Our little group assembled in the mess hall for breakfast, and a short time later we drove off through the shifting fog, following muddy roads across the island to Constantine Harbor.

Riding at anchor on the gentle waves were two small boats. One was a new fiber-glass skiff. The other was an old gray dory named *Dipper,* famed for its years of travel around the Aleutian Islands. The crew finished loading large plywood boxes into both boats. Soon the shoreline dissolved behind us in the fog.

Our crew, Nick Nevzoroff and Cyril Kudrin, seemed to know precisely where we were. I took comfort in the knowledge that their Aleut ancestors had successfully plied these waters for thousands of years. Occasionally, tall black rocks emerged from the fog and provided Nick with landmarks. He glanced a few times at his compass but seldom found it necessary to correct his course.

Fifteen minutes later we moved slowly into a large, protected bay and began working our way through a bed of kelp that lay in long brown strands on the surface. Ahead of the boat a sea otter popped up and promptly dived again. Murres, puffins, and gulls passed back and forth, emerging from the fog and promptly losing themselves from view again. Then a brilliant red plastic float, as big as a bushel basket, took shape on the ocean's surface. It marked the end of the first net. The evening before, its small white floats had been suspended in an orderly line across the kelp bed. But a dozen or more of those once neatly spaced floats were now tangled and knotted.

We could see the otters almost as soon as the net was in view. They stood straight up in the water — as high as they could on their webbed hind feet — and watched the boat coming steadily closer. Burdened by the cords of the net, they dived clumsily, reappeared, then dived again, each time tangling the net still more. Nick grinned. "Got three."

Freeing an enraged and frightened 50-pound sea otter from a tangle of nylon netting is no simple chore. Cyril pulled the net to the boat and reached for the first otter just as it reached for him. Its mouth was open wide, its head twisted to one side, and those rows of teeth — capable of crushing shellfish — were snapping at Cyril's gloved hand. Nick took a burlap bag stuffed with old netting and used it to hold the otter's head aside as he picked away at the net.

Then the otter was grabbed by a hind leg and swiftly lifted into one of the crates, head down. The screened lid slapped quickly into place and was secured. Inside the box, the otter squealed a loud, shrill protest.

With the first three captives of the morning aboard, Nick and Cyril turned back for the harbor with a load. For them the day had only begun. The two crews continued to check nets, and two hours after

Two Amchitka sea otters being netted for transfer to a new home. *George Laycock*

they started, they had brought back the day's catch of ten sea otters. The otters had made the first step in a long trip.

Some weeks earlier a letter from the project leader, John Vania, in charge of the state of Alaska's marine mammal research, had brought me details of his summer plans for the sea otters. The otter trapping was scheduled for Amchitka, a 42-mile-long island far out in the Aleutians. John expected to fly to Amchitka on June 17th. He would have his trapping operation in full swing a week later. As fast as he could catch and process a planeload of otters, he would ship them back to release points along the Alaska coast where there is good otter territory — but few or no otters. "I'll fill you in on the other details," he said, "when you get up here."

His trapping went even better than he expected. In less than a week he had the first load of 38 healthy sea otters in holding tanks on Amchitka. And the day I arrived in Anchorage, John was already aboard a plane coming back toward the mainland with his valued cargo. The plane, chartered by the Atomic Energy Commission, touched down in Sitka in southeastern Alaska. Each of the otters had traveled in an individual crate specially designed to hold a few inches of water for the health and comfort of these pampered passengers. All arrived in excellent condition.

John Vania had made the journey warmly dressed against the constant 48-degree temperature maintained for the comfort of the sea otters.

Waiting to meet the larger plane at Sitka was an amphibious Grumman Goose. In this plane John shuttled the otters a few at a time on the final leg of their journey, a ten-minute flight to Klag Bay. Each time the plane came to rest, John opened the otter boxes, one at a time, tipped them up, and watched the new residents slide into the cold clear water. They popped to the surface curiously to observe the men and the plane moving across the bay.

Later that night, back in Anchorage where he lives, John Vania talked with me about his otter project. "This animal is something special," he said with obvious feeling. "And it almost didn't make it. That's why we think this work is important. And as for Amchitka," he added, "it's hard to tell what's going to happen to that island and the wildlife there now, so we want to move as many of the sea otters as we can. You'll see how we handle them when you get out there. Next week is my week to stay here and work in the office, but we have two other biologists, Ed Klinkhart and

Karl Schneider, out there. Both of them have had a lot of experience with otters."

Once before I had observed sea otters in the wild. With my son Mike, I was driving one morning along the coast of California. South of Monterey we saw a wooden sign beside the highway marking Point Lobos State Reserve. We followed the narrow, twisting lane through the park to the edge of the Pacific. Frolicking within 30 feet of shore, was my first sea otter. During the day we saw at least four others. There, as in Alaska, sea otters had once been abundant.

That was before the fateful year of 1741. That year Vitus Bering, a Danish explorer commanding a Russian ship, sailed eastward to Alaska, and his party became the first white explorers to see these amazing animals. The two ships he commanded became separated; the one Bering was aboard ran ashore in the Commander Islands off the Kamchatka Peninsula and split apart in the shallows. During the winter Bering died, but the surviving crewmen assembled a makeshift boat from salvaged materials. They returned to Russia, taking along several hundred of the fabulous furs of the sea otters they had discovered in such abundance around the Aleutians.

Sea otter fur was an immediate success. Soon other ships sailed out of Russian ports to bring back more otter pelts. As long as the sea otters lasted, the pillage went on. The native Stone Age Aleuts were pressed into service catching and killing the otters. And along the Pacific Coast, all the way to southern California, the otters were mercilessly cleaned out.

By 1867, having taken hundreds of thousands of pelts and all but eliminating the once abundant sea otters, the Russians saw little future for Alaska. That year ownership of that vast land passed to the United States at a cost of about two cents an acre.

With this change in ownership, American fur hunters took up

where their Russian counterparts had left off. Their methodical carnage came tragically close to bringing to extinction one of the earth's most amazing fur bearers. By 1900 many people were convinced that the sea otter was already gone. Today it is believed the numbers might have been down to fewer than 500, those living in small pods hidden from the hunters in remote coves. In 1911, when many thought it was already too late to help, four nations, the United States, Japan, Russia, and Canada, reached an international agreement that protected sea otters from further commercial hunting. Two years later the President of the United States signed an executive order establishing the Aleutian Islands National Wildlife Refuge.

Among the biggest of all the national wildlife refuges, this string of islands is a wonderfully wild national treasure, rich in scenery — except where man has littered and abused it — and harboring abundant and varied wild creatures.

Once they had been offered protection from the ruthless hunting of the fur merchants, Alaska's sea otters began a gradual recovery. Far to the south, meanwhile, a hidden southern race of the "extinct" animals slowly built up their population, and in 1938 a group of 94 sea otters was discovered swimming in the kelp beds at the mouth of Bixby Creek near Monterey. Today there are an estimated 700 to 800 along the California coast. But this remnant population hangs on by a thin thread, threatened constantly because they compete with fishermen for the commercially important abalone.

Mrs. Nathaniel Owings of Big Sur, who has led the fight in behalf of that isolated otter population, is especially concerned because the California otters, which should increase their population by about fifteen percent annually, are apparently decreasing instead. In the ten-year period between 1957 and 1967, a sea otter census along the California coast showed the count sliding from 638 to 562.

To conservationists, there is little question about one major cause for this decline. The otters' troubles became serious with new state regulations permitting the abalone industry to ship its shellfish out of California. This increased the demand. Prices went up. Consequently the number of commercial fishermen getting into the abalone industry increased. With the growing pressure on the resource, the supply of commercial-sized abalone decreased.

At this point the commercial fishermen, searching for something to blame, decided the sea otter was their culprit, although how much abalone the sea otters really do eat can vary, depending on the availability of abalone, sea urchins, and perhaps some other potential foods.

California decided on an experimental transplant of twenty sea otters about 60 miles to the north in an effort to move them away from the abalone. This solution was first advocated by a state politician. Even the most skilled otter experts have a percentage of their captives die during the netting and handling. Around Amchitka, with its overpopulation of sea otters, this loss does not threaten the future of the entire population. But where the population totals only 1000 or so animals, any significant losses could be devastating. The mortality could run as high or higher than 40 percent.

There is not much doubt that abalone fishermen shoot sea otters in direct violation of laws that make the offense punishable by heavy fines and jail sentences. In testimony during one hearing, Mrs. Owings wondered aloud why the sea otter population of California continues to fall instead of rise. Fishermen present decided a finger was being pointed at them and became incensed. One pointed out that sea otters were hard to shoot from a bobbing boat. Another added that if you shoot a sea otter in the head it floats; shot elsewhere, he insisted, it sinks. It is common knowledge that dead sea otters wash up on the California beaches bearing the marks of knives. Some of these specimens have been mounted and displayed, including one bearing fourteen knife wounds.

All things considered, the future of the sea otter along the coast of California is not bright. And Mrs. Owings, from her home at Big Sur, has organized a "Friends of the Sea Otter" group to promote research and fight the cause of the endangered southern population.

Meanwhile, otters have prospered in the Aleutians. Gradually they have spread out from the little remnants that escaped the hunters to reoccupy locations where the Russians found them. They have reached Attu and other islands out at the far end of the Aleutians. As they continue to increase, they threaten their own food supplies, and this is what happened around Amchitka. Marine mammal biologist Karl W. Kenyon of the U.S. Fish and Wildlife Service noted that the sea otters had reached the carrying capacity of their Amchitka range by about 1943. Their population declined, and the average weight fell. Eighty- and 90-pound adult male sea otters are common in some areas. But around Amchitka the biologists seldom weigh one of more than 70 pounds.

Sea otters deserve a better shake than they've had at the hands of humans down through the years. After a few days on Amchitka I could readily appreciate John Vania's statement that "this animal is something special."

Unlike other marine mammals, the otter is not equipped with a thick layer of insulating fat. Instead, he has only his luxurious fur coat to keep him warm. If water should penetrate the fur and chill the otter, slim indeed are his chances of survival. When Ed Klinkhart or Karl Schneider noticed one of the animals shivering in its holding tank, he made a mental note that the number on hand for shipping had been reduced by one.

There are 230 animals shown in this aerial view
of a pod of Aleutian sea otters. *Karl W. Kenyon*

"The heat regulatory mechanism of the sea otter," Bob Jones,
manager of the Aleutian Islands National Wildlife Refuge, told me,
"operates in a narrowly limited range, and absolute cleanliness is
the key." If the otter's amazing fur gets soiled, it cannot insulate
its wearer. In an environment where cleanliness is essential to
survival, the sea otter has evolved into one of the world's most serious
preeners and natural hairdressers. When not feeding or sleeping, they
are working at the perpetual task of cleaning their fur. I watched
them in the holding tanks and in the bays, busily grooming them-

selves. They can reach every part of their bodies, even rolling into a tight ball to rub their backs where it would seem impossible for their short arms to reach. The otter's coat fits him as if it were two sizes too large, and this is apparently an aid in keeping it clean. I watched one afternoon as a preening otter caught a fold of his coat and scrubbed it between the flat pads of his front feet.

So seriously does the otter work at scratching, rubbing, and preening that human observers sometimes start to scratch as they watch. Yet according to the best guesses of the biologists, the sea otter, which has no external parasites, doesn't itch at all.

In Juneau one day I had an opportunity to examine closely the pelt taken from a sea otter. The fur is incredibly dense, and so soft the hand seems to float in it. It traps beneath its surface a layer of air which is excellent insulation. And the pelt is big; a sea otter is about three times as heavy as his inland cousin, the river otter. The body of the sea otter is bulkier and less streamlined, more like his neighbors the seals than his sleek mainland relatives.

Motive power for the sea otter comes from his hind feet, which have evolved into flippers. Often I've wished for a slow-motion movie of his actions. Clumsy and stumbling when on the land, he moves with incredible beauty in the water. Like liquid fur, he turns end-over-end, or rolls so smoothly and gracefully that the motion is difficult for the human eye to follow. For a few minutes an otter will lie motionless on his back, his broad hind flippers and his short tail trailing out behind. Then he moves one flipper, or seemingly no flipper at all, and folds in the water to slip from sight without a splash or scarcely a ripple to mark the place. He may double over and surface again facing the opposite direction. Or he will execute a combination of maneuvers until you never know for certain which way he will move next.

The front legs are short, and the small paws flat and heavily padded. They are useful for collecting and holding food, grooming the fur, or for a female to clasp her pup to her chest.

Sea otters are big eaters. It is common for them to consume a quarter of their weight a day in seafoods. In the week before Vania shipped out his first 1968 planeload of captives, they consumed more than a ton of fine fish fillets, shipped for them from Seattle in large frozen blocks and served up four times daily.

Aside from man, few creatures have ever learned to use tools. But the sea otter has. One day in southern California I stood watching a sea otter floating on its back among the kelp strands. He swam slowly on the gentle waves, busily working with a shellfish carried on his upturned belly. He was having trouble with the shellfish. Repeatedly he grasped it between his front paws, lifted it straight above his chest as high as his short arms would permit, and promptly brought it crashing down against his body. But through my binoculars I could see that he held a flat rock on his chest. He was using the rock to crack the shellfish so he could obtain the meat. I had heard of this, but for the first time I observed it myself. Apparently this use of Stone Age tools is more common among California sea otters than among their northern cousins.

Some naturalists even think the sea otter may use rocks to help him break shellfish off the ocean floor. Whatever his methods, he can harvest abalone — a prized shellfish that human fishermen break off submerged rocks by using tire tools.

Sea otters sometimes come out of the ocean and rest on the rocky ledges just above the water's edge. But most of their life is spent in the water. It is here on the surface that they sleep and mate, but they are believed to bear their young on the rocks. The sleeping sea otter drifts on his back. The ocean is his mattress, and sometimes

A mother sea otter and pup surprised by the photographer. *Karl W. Kenyon*

a strip of kelp draped across his chest is all that keeps him from floating out with the tide.

There is no special breeding season among sea otters, and consequently young of various ages may be seen at any time. Most pups, however, are born during summer — about eight months after the mating — and are completely dependent upon their mothers.

For perhaps a year the female nurses the pup and carries it around with her. The female sea otter is famous for her qualities of motherhood; even if her pup should die, she may carry it around for a week or more. There are lessons the female must teach her pup, including how to swim and how to fish. When very young, the otter pup cannot sink. If his mother should leave him topside and dive for food, the pup may try to follow, but for all his mad paddling and splashing, he finds it impossible to dive.

Back on the surface, floating on her back with her pup draped across her stomach, the mother feeds herself and carefully brushes the scraps off her fur. While feeding, both mother and pup may do a log roll, surface again, and shake their heads as if refreshed by their dip.

Sometimes the female sea otter will leave her pup sleeping briefly on his back in the water, a strand of kelp draped across his middle. It may be that the bald eagle overhead takes an occasional otter pup at such a time. I talked with an engineer on Amchitka who reports seeing an eagle snatch a pup from the rocks where it had come out with its mother. The eagle, overloaded from the beginning, struggled a few feet until the pup cleared the ground, but then had to drop its prize — apparently uninjured — back on the rocks and fly away defeated.

As he is learning to feed, a sea otter often comes up with rocks. But he learns to tell the edibles from the inedibles and acquires other fine points of otter behavior — to become independent at last of the mother's solicitous care.

Once the sea otter has matured, it is likely to join a pod of other otters segregated according to their sex. The males and females may have their individual beaches on which they haul out to rest and preen. Best known of such areas on Amchitka are two beaches named St. Makarius West, where the females congregate, and St. Makarius East, which is male country. To John Vania and his co-workers these places are the "Grandma and Grandpa beaches."

There are an estimated 3000 sea otters living in the bays around Amchitka Island. This is perhaps a tenth of the world population and one of the biggest concentrations of sea otters anywhere. But even though they are abundant in a few places, and are no longer endangered creatures in Alaskan waters, sea otters probably occupy only about 20 percent of their original range. In Alaska alone, there probably is suitable habitat for twice the present number. The largest areas of unoccupied sea otter habitat remaining in the state, according to Vania, lie in the southeastern section. Here the Russians found their last major hunting spot; after 1900, no longer were there any confirmed reports of sea otters being found there.

As a beginning, in 1965 and 1966, the Alaska Department of Fish and Game brought in and released 43 otters from Prince William Sound in the Klag Bay area, and some of them have since been slghted there. The efforts of 1968 were designed to bolster that population and assure its success.

Biologists confronted with the task of capturing, processing, and transplanting the otters first had to devise suitable methods. Before statehood — when Alaska took over otter management — the U.S. Bureau of Sport Fisheries and Wildlife made pioneering transplant efforts. The method of capture was to sneak up on unsuspecting otters where they had come ashore and try to capture them in a dip net before they could dive back into the water. Sometimes it worked, but more often it failed. It was most effective during heavy storms, which sometimes forced the otters out of the water and which helped to distract them.

Early in 1951, when bitter winter winds were whipping across the Aleutians, the U.S. Fish and Wildlife Service vessel *Brown Bear* left the refuge headquarters at Cold Bay, headed for Amchitka. Aboard was refuge manager Bob Jones and his crew. Jones planned to capture sea otters for transplanting to other islands. No one had ever attempted this before. No one knew whether otters could be kept alive in captivity, or how best to care for them. The crew set up its camp on the shores of Amchitka, and began chasing otters around the rocks with their nets. On the slippery tidal rocks they captured 35 otters during the month of March. They installed them in shallow lakes with mud bottoms, but the otters died. Obviously, transplanting sea otters was going to be far more difficult than those pioneering workers had expected.

During the next few years the biologists postponed their efforts to transplant otters while they further studied the rare animals. Veterinarians joined the Fish and Wildlife Service biologists on some of their Amchitka study trips. Biologist Karl W. Kenyon devoted a large part of his work during those years to the efforts to perfect the right system for keeping the delicate, captive sea otters vigorous.

Finally, on May 20, 1959, a Fish and Wildlife Service plane carrying seven yearling otters and a crew of concerned refuge workers left Amchitka for the Pribilof Islands. The plane was flown at altitudes below 2000 feet for the otters' safety, and cabin temperatures were held below 50 degrees. Even then the animals were too warm. The crew sprinkled their furs with water and gave them drinking water directly from bottles. For the first time a shipment of sea otters arrived at the release point in excellent condition. Although the transplant was considered a success, the number released was probably too small to build permanent populations of otters around the Pribilofs. But a start had been made. Vania's crew of state workers could eventually follow up with much bigger transplants.

Biologists from both agencies continued to work closely and pool their ideas and experience. "You should have seen some of the things we have rigged up for this work," Ed Klinkhart told me. "We thought we might capture them with a cannon net the way they do waterfowl or wild turkeys. We set it up on the beach where the otters haul out. But they wouldn't come out where we could shoot the net over them. Then we tried baiting the area with clams, and that wouldn't work either. We tried running up on them in a skiff and scooping them out with a dip net, but they could easily outmaneuver us."

At one point biologists tried an ingenious type of sunken trap. They built an open-top cage out of pipes. Then they attached floats to it. But to sink it beneath the surface, they weighted it down. The plan: to wait until an unsuspecting otter swam over the trap, then release the weight with a string and have the trap float to the surface, catching the otter inside. "The only trouble with it," Klinkhart admitted, "was that it didn't work.

"We had tried about everything we could think of. We could sometimes run down a few otters when they would come out on the beaches, but not often enough. Then we began thinking about the old methods used by the native Aleuts. One thing they had used was a net. We went to Cordova and bought a king salmon net and took the leads off it. The first time we set the net, we caught an otter before it was two-thirds out. And we had five more right away." Nets became the standard otter-catching equipment, and last summer biologists set fifteen nets, each 300 feet long.

Once, as I rode with Nick and Cyril, we came upon a net with four struggling otters. We had only three crates along. The otter catchers put an animal in each of the boxes, then looked around for a way to carry the fourth. They spotted the big dip net. We made it back to Constantine Harbor with the otter slung comfortably in a hammock made by suspending the net between the side of the boat and one of the boxes. He probably had the softest ride of anyone aboard.

On most such trips out to the nets, we saw legions of sea birds coming through the fog on whistling wings, or peeling off their clifftop perches. On the rocky ledges nested glaucous-winged gulls, cormorants, and thick-billed murres. The rocks were capped with carpets of rich green vegetation, and in the shallow soil at the clifftops horned puffins had their nesting tunnels. When startled, they sometimes hurled themselves off and gained speed as they came toward the ocean below in a long gliding arch. Then they would level off and speed past us, stubby wings beating so fast they looked like propellers whirling around and around the birds' short, stout bodies. Small groups of eiders flew at startling speed close to the waves and passed from view, while pigeon guillemots rode the seas at safe distances. Sea otters frequently popped up in the kelp beds, and sometimes there was a harbor seal.

When we were still a mile or more from the harbor, Nick flicked on the microphone of his portable radio and talked briefly with Ed Klinkhart. At the beach Ed was waiting for us with his pickup truck. The heavy wooden boxes with the otters inside were quickly transferred to the truck and hauled past the old World War II ship dock to the far corner of a big warehouse which provides the sea otter crew a place to mend nets and maintain its records, free of the wind and rain.

They worked fast to transfer the otters from their boxes to the big holding tanks. First, however, Ed or Karl would check and record the sex of each otter and quickly decorate one hind flipper with a numbered Monel metal clamp tag. Then the otter was weighed, with two men quickly carrying it off to slide into the water of the holding tank.

In the early days of their work with captive sea otters, Vania and his co-workers built a floating live-box with screen sides in which to hold otters awaiting transfer. The advantage was that a constant supply of fresh water washed through it. But on Amchitka, the rough seas would likely have dashed the live-box against the rocks; the seas there are often so rough the crew could not have reached the box at all.

The answer was an above-ground swimming pool, designed by the otter trappers and supplied with fresh seawater by pumps. Last summer Vania's crew had four of these holding tanks in use. Each one measures 16 by 24 feet and holds three feet of water. Walkways a few inches above the water provide resting-places on which the

The sea otter, although no longer threatened with extinction, still occupies only about 20 percent of its original range. *George Laycock*

otters haul out. Individual pumps constantly supply each tank with fresh salt water. "We drain the tanks and clean them every three or four days," Ed told me. Around the top of each tank is a three-foot fence of strong wire mesh to prevent otters from crawling over and out. Fifteen otters is the most biologists like to hold in a tank at one time.

Sea otters, nervous and defensive when first taken, soon calm down. They tame readily and the least nervous among them would probably take food from the human hand if anyone cared to try feeding them in that manner. During my Amchitka stay I visited the otter holding tanks whenever time permitted. There was always an intriguing show underway there.

One morning, as one of the boats returned with a new load of otters, I was waiting at the tank to photograph the transfer. Among the captives were two females with pups. It frequently happens that a female and pup are taken together. Sea otter mothers keep their young so close to them that it is difficult to imagine how one might be taken and the other escape. The crew brought the first female and her pup back in separate boxes because they would have to weigh and check them separately, and under stress the female might injure her pup. I asked Ed if she would accept the young once they were in the tank. "She will go right over and get him," he said confidently.

The two boxes tipped up at the same moment. The old otter slid gracefully into the water and her youngster took a belly smacker like a kid in a farm pond. The female rushed to where the young otter was and tenderly gathered him up and held him. Swimming on her back, she clasped him on her chest with both arms, all the while looking around nervously at this strange setting and the men there. Then she took her pup to the far corner of the tank and crowded with him among the other otters.

Soon she calmed down. Occasionally she would roll over in the water, still clasping her pup, and come to rest again on her back. Once, while she floated with her pup, she patted him gently with one paw, as a human mother might do to calm her child. Whether or not she does this to reassure the young otter, no man can know for certain. I asked biologist Karl Schneider if he would care to interpret this action of the female sea otter. "I would prefer," he said smilingly, "not to."

Sea otters are sociable creatures, and where there is one there are usually several more. Their territories are believed to be small. In the wild, they may grow old near the place of their birth. Karl Kenyon once recaptured two sea otters two years after they had been tagged, and they were within three miles of the place he had first taken them.

Alaskans are not alone in their desire to see the sea otter come back to its historic territories. Some of the largest of the original populations were along the Canadian coast. The heart of a once flourishing commercial trade in otters was along the rocky coast of Vancouver Island. In 1778 Captain James Cook visited Nootka Sound, and afterward the otter hunters descended on that area. After 1909 there were never again any wild sea otters reported from Nootka Island. And none was seen anywhere along the British Columbia coast after 1929.

During 1967 British Columbia held a series of meetings which brought provincial authorities and conservation workers to Victoria to make plans for bringing the sea otter back to Canada. "The purpose of our reintroduction," they said, "is simply to reestablish this biologically and historically unique mammal to its rightful place in the Canadian fauna; the economic value of sea otter furs is of secondary importance." The thousand miles of unoccupied territory that lies between this Canadian habitat and the Alaskan otter populations make it obvious that sea otters would not reach the Vancouver Island region by natural dispersion for a long time.

Next, Canadians sought to choose the best of their sea otter country. The U.S. Fish and Wildlife Service sent marine mammal biologist Karl Kenyon up from Seattle to join British Columbia biologist Don Blood, who was in charge of the budding otter transplant program. For five days, in June 1967, they made low-level flight inspections of the entire coast of British Columbia. Based on his experience in the Aleutians, Kenyon was encouraged by what he and Blood saw along this coast. Some of the localities they had inspected looked to Kenyon like "ideal habitat."

The stage for the transfer had been further set by the application of British Columbia for 25 otters and Alaska's granting of the permit. This shipment was to come from the 250 to 300 otters that biologists hoped to trap around Amchitka during the summer of 1968. The release point chosen was Bunsby Island, whose rocky coves had once resounded to the shots of the sea otter merchants. Many factors favor this spot. There is a lack of pollution. The area is isolated from boat traffic, industry, and human population centers; and there is an abundant supply of choice sea otter foods.

Everything seemed in order and the Canadians had even assigned their 177-foot fisheries research vessel, the *G. B. Reed,* to make the two-week trip and pick up the otters. They were to be transported in large tanks through which fresh seawater would be circulated. As it turned out, this sea voyage for man and otter could have been avoided because the AEC plane could have taken the otters to southern Alaska, where they could have been transferred to the Canadians.

But August — when the transfer was to be made — came and went, and British Columbia did not get its sea otters. With abundant stock apparently available, I wondered why this excellent coastal range should be denied. Was it AEC's decision? "They're Alaska's sea otters," said a representative of that agency, "and we don't care what they do with them. We just supply the transportation to other parts of Alaska, and if the state wants to transfer some of them to another country, it doesn't matter to us."

The only remaining possibility was that this decision had been made by Alaskans — and, I suspected, those at the highest level of state government. A few weeks later I asked Alaska's then Governor Walter J. Hickel why British Columbia had not received otters in 1968. It was, he told me, a policy decision to see that none went elsewhere until all parts of Alaska that could be restocked with otters had them, and that eventually Canada would get its otters. Some conservationists are convinced that, if first things were to be put first in the long-range welfare of the sea otters, all possible surpluses from overpopulated areas such as Amchitka would be used primarily to restock suitable areas — whether inside or outside the state of Alaska. The world of fashion could surely wait that long. British Columbia has since received sea otters from Alaska. Others have been transplanted to Oregon.

Meanwhile, Alaska is attempting to rejuvenate the sea otter fur industry. On January 30, 1968, more than 100 fur brokers from around the world congregated in the Seattle Fur Exchange to bid on sea otter pelts for the first legal sale in 57 years. It was a big day for Alaska and a fitting testimony to the prolonged efforts to save the coveted sea otter from extinction. Biologists believe Alaska can safely take at least 500 pelts a year.

On that day, Alaska offered the pelts of 920 otters, all expertly graded and divided according to size and coloring into lots averaging five pelts each. Some of the pelts had been "harvested" by biologists from the overpopulated herds around Amchitka as early as 1962 and held in cold storage. The method of taking them is with a .243-caliber rifle from shore. Dead sea otters float, and they can be picked up from skiffs.

Alaska officials were pleased with the reception given their glamour furs after the long absence from the market. The average price per pelt was $161.24. They ranged from a low of $40 each to a high of $2300. The top price was paid by Neiman-Marcus Co. of Dallas, which planned to stitch the skins into a coat, destined no doubt to become a status symbol.

From its overpopulated otter areas, Alaska expects to take at least 500 furs a year for the market. The otters are taken by state employees seeking out the older individuals and avoiding injury to females, especially those with young. Selected for the "harvest site" in 1968 were Tanaga, Kanaga, and Adak islands, all of which have otter herds that have reached population peaks and begun to decline. Normally, otter populations, increasing at a rate of fifteen percent a year, build to a high point around an island, then fall off sharply as surplus stock moves off to populate some nearby area. Alaska biologists precede any taking of fur animals with a preseason survey. This is generally the task of Karl Schneider who, along with a local helper, spends enough weeks with a herd to be certain that the planned harvest is lower than the annual rate of increase. Although the shooting of the frolicsome sea otters may be no more appealing today than it was a century and a half ago, it is considered sound wildlife management.

During the summer of 1968 Vania and his co-workers had even greater success than they had expected. A month after he first reached Amchitka, Vania had supervised the trapping and moving of more than 250 sea otters to southeastern Alaska. By the end of the summer he had transferred a total of 302 to that section of Alaska and then made a final shipment for the year of 57 to the Pribilofs.

Large parts of the sea otter's original range, according to the beliefs of Karl Kenyon, will probably never again support otters because of pollution and human concentrations. Hopefully, all those pockets of coastal North America where the amazing sea otter could survive once more will someday have new flourishing populations of them. The amazing element in the saga of the sea otter is that it is still among the living species. For the otter, swimming out there on his back or popping up in the kelp beds to view the intruding human, the future looks better than at any time since the days of Vitus Bering.

7

Oil and
the North Slope

THE SNOWCAPPED PEAKS of the fabled Brooks Range of Arctic Alaska stood in bold saw-toothed splendor against the gray summer sky. Below us the rushing waters of the Alatna River led into a canyon reaching toward the crest of the ridge. But a deep blanket of clouds had scudded in from the northwest. The clouds flowed around the steep slopes, choked off our route, and hid the valley ahead.

Our pilot reluctantly banked the single-engine craft eastward. Successful bush pilots are compromisers. Those who fly in the Arctic learn to yield to the weather, not to fight it. So after several miles we rounded a high-rise peak, to follow the twisting course of the John River upward toward the village at Anaktuvuk Pass on the crest of the divide. The 115 residents of Anaktuvuk are all that remain of the once nomadic Nuniamuit, who until recent times roamed the Brooks Range following the caribou herds.

Gradually the river grew smaller. A thousand little streams split from the mother current and vanished in deep-walled canyons to gather the new water from fields of slowly melting snow. Then, by looking straight down, I could see that the streams now were flowing north instead of south.

Along the Anaktuvuk River we had entered the wilderness of the North Slope where, in the brief weeks of summer, caribou come to bear their calves, shorebirds return from beyond the equator to build their flimsy nests, and men with oil on their minds come with their rumbling machines. These were the elements of the modern Arctic tapestry that had lured me northward thousands of miles. In the two years that had passed since the discovery of oil at Prudhoe Bay, the Arctic had become a land of frenzied human activity. And *Audubon* had sent me back to Alaska to see what had happened to the North Slope.

We flew for some time through canyons surrounded by peaks, because the Brooks Range is not a single flank of mountains standing between interior Alaska and the North Slope. Instead, this northern terminus of the Rocky Mountains is a 100-mile-wide band of upturned real estate. The frigid Arctic Ocean, not yet in view, still lay 50 or 60 miles north of us.

Along the Arctic Slope the mean annual temperature ranges between 10 and 15 degrees Fahrenheit, and winter lows may fall to 50 degrees or more below zero. Winter locks the land and sea in a massive block of ice. The land is dry as well as cold across this Arctic desert. The annual precipitation of four to eight inches is less than in parts of the desert lands of the American Southwest.

But below us the arrival of spring had turned the tundra into a soggy sponge. The snow blanket was melting and the plains were pockmarked with odd-shaped pools of ice water. Below the surface, the everlasting layer of permafrost, 1300 feet thick in some places, formed a watertight seal that kept the water from percolating into the earth. In spring the melting snow first fills all the pools, then slowly overflows to follow nearly invisible channels toward the sea.

With winter gone, the foothills and the coastal plains come to life.

South of Point Barrow, the undisturbed tundra with its
meandering rivers and small lakes. *Josef Muench*

At Point Barrow on the coast, the northernmost settlement in North
America, the sun does not set from May 10th to August 2nd. Arctic
plants soon become tinged with green, then suddenly flourish, and
in the continuous light of the summer weeks, rush ahead in re-
markable growth. Brilliant flowers on dwarf plants carpet the tundra
with reds, purples, whites, and yellows.

Down from the hills come the caribou cows, heavy with calf,
traveling age-old routes to their fawning grounds. Alaska's two
largest herds of caribou live on these plains at least part of the year.

In the western portion of the North Slope is the Arctic herd, numbering 300,000 head. To the east, the Porcupine herd, with 140,000 head, spends its winters in Canada but crosses back into Alaska for the spring and summer. The ancient fawning grounds of these two herds overlap in the central part of the state's northern coastal plains, in the heart of the newly discovered oil fields between the Colville and Canning Rivers.

Sharing the tundra with the deer is a wealth of birds, back from distant parts of the world to raise their young in the seasonal abundance. Shorebirds and songbirds of many varieties arrive with eiders, scoters, pintails, and loons. Wildlife observers have recorded 171 species of birds on Alaska's North Slope.

But this is a big land of mountains, foothills, and coastal plains — spread across the cap of the continent for 76,000 miles — and the wildlife, though abundant, is often widely scattered.

We flew on over precipitous mountains toward the rolling foothills of the Brooks Range, rising 600 to 3500 feet and blending to the north into a gently sloping tableland that is slightly above sea level and, in some places, nearly 100 miles across. Along the coast are three native villages with populations totaling perhaps 2500. In addition to the natives, there are a few military outposts on the North Slope.

Plus 2000 oilmen.

The smell of oil is not new to the North Slope. Early explorers mushing across northern Alaska found places where oil seeped from the earth in plain view. The locations of such seeps were known, and this evidence drew the early attention of the U.S. Geological Survey. For two decades following the turn of the current century the Geological Survey dispatched small scientific parties to map the region and explore it for potential oil.

They learned enough to attract the attention of the navy. In 1923 President Warren G. Harding, by executive order, carved out a section of the Arctic about the size of Indiana and proclaimed it Naval Petroleum Reserve Number 4, which present-day Alaskans refer to as "Pet Four." This reserve lies in the central portion of the coastal plain between Point Lay and the Colville River and reaches from the Arctic Ocean inland as far as 250 miles.

Tucked away in its northeastern corner, Alaska has perhaps its least damaged wilderness, the 8,900,000-acre Arctic National Wildlife Range. And between "Pet Four" and the Wildlife Range is that section of the coastal plain which includes Prudhoe Bay and which recently has gained world fame — especially among the swashbuckling forces of the oil industry. On to the west of "Pet Four" is more coastal land that is being scoured for new evidence of oil and coal reserves, and there the state of Alaska hopes to lease additional land to the oil and mining companies.

After the Geological Survey came the U.S. Navy which, during the 1940's, conducted its own exploration program. The navy did more than map oil seeps in "Pet Four" and note outcroppings of promising rock formations. It began drilling test wells. By 1955 it had punched 37 such holes into the perpetually frozen earth. In the process it discovered oil fields at Fish Creek, Simpson, and Umiat, the latter village a grubby and littered all-male settlement on the banks of the Colville River. In its searching the navy also located natural gas fields. But except for tapping some of the reservoirs of gas to bring its conveniences to a navy installation and to local Eskimos, these riches have not been brought into production. The major reason has always been the same problem which plagues oil producers there today — the difficulty of moving the oil to market.

Still, the exploratory work of the navy was not lost on the oil industry, whose geologists and executives were more convinced than ever that great reserves of crude oil lay locked beneath the Arctic. During the 1960's a number of wells were drilled, none of them promising and each of them costing staggering sums of stockholders' money. Among the leaders were the Atlantic Richfield Company and Humble Oil & Refining Company. But the high cost of unproductive holes punched through the permafrost slowed the Arctic treasure hunt.

Eventually the drilling rigs dwindled to a single unit working its way through the formations of the North Slope at Prudhoe Bay. Then in March of 1968, Atlantic Richfield and Humble Oil began test drilling on their jointly held Sag River State No. 1 site. This was the rig that was to awaken the giant. A few months later, in the summer of 1968, came the announcement of discovered oil. Estimates of these reserves have run from 10 to 15 billion barrels, with then Secretary of the Interior Walter J. Hickel predicting that yields could go to 100 billion barrels or more. The jubilant oil industry proclaimed this to be one of the greatest oil strikes in history.

Almost overnight, oil companies with North Slope holdings rushed to renew their explorations. The Prudhoe Bay region had become oil country, and the problems of engineering, economics, and ecology on the North Slope all took on staggering proportions. Alaska's impoverished state government was suddenly knighted by King Midas.

In Anchorage on September 10, 1969, Alaska opened oil company bids on state lands to be leased on the Arctic Slope. Included were 179 tracts totaling 450,858 acres. Practically every important oil company in the country was on hand with its sealed bids, and when the day's totals were tallied, Alaska had been enriched by a windfall

An exploratory oil rig on the North Slope. *Mobil Oil*

of more than $900,000,000. In addition, Alaska will receive income
from royalties and taxes on oil pumped — calculated at $200 to $250
million annually.

As you fly out across the coastal plains today you can, on a clear
day, see the oil rigs from miles away, standing stark and lonely-
looking against the gray-white landscape. Clustered around each rig
are all of the elements required for the crew to live and carry out
its task. Giant collapsible tanks hold stores of fuel and drilling
compounds. House trailers are grouped to make living quarters.
Heavy-wheeled trucks rumble around on short roads that seem to

go nowhere. Each camp has its own kitchen, recreational facility, and generator.

Rugged, experienced oilmen from Oklahoma and Texas man these outposts. As we flew around one site I saw two men staring up at us. There is deep suspicion of any low-flying aircraft. Each drilling operation is highly secretive, with owners taking elaborate precautions to hide what they are doing. For example, oil firms send in skilled spies to study the other companies' operations from low-flying helicopters. Aerial photographs are used to analyze the competition's activities. Sometimes a company will order equipment or supplies it has no intention of using, and stack the decoy equipment out in plain view to throw off the calculations of the oil spies.

Spread over these oil fields are plant communities woven into a protective rug of tundra that insulates the permafrost from the summer warmth and allows the earth to thaw only to depths ranging from a few inches to a few feet at most. Anyone working in the Arctic knows that the tundra is fragile and easily broken. Once ruptured, the tundra loses its insulating properties. Where vehicle tracks cut the tundra, the permafrost is exposed to greater warming and begins to thaw. Decades or perhaps centuries will pass before tundra, scarred by vehicle tracks in summer, heals. In the tundra of Amchitka Island in the Aleutians, I have seen the tracks of World War II vehicles unchanged after a quarter of a century. In the Seward Peninsula there is a set of wagon tracks which an aging miner recalled from 1920. The trail where the wagon ran across the tundra only twice is still unhealed after 50 years.

Adding to the complexity of this problem for both engineer and ecologist is the fact that the nature of permafrost varies from place to place. The larger the percentage of ice crystals in permafrost, the less solid it becomes, and on sloping land it has a tendency to slide as it thaws. To protect the permafrost on building sites calls for covering it with thick foundations of gravel, usually dug from stream beds. Millions of tons of gravel will be needed to build roads, camps, and drill sites on the North Slope.

From the air, with the snows of last winter melting, we could see more graphically than from the ground what the oil operations had done to the tundra. Vehicle tracks run in every direction. Why a set of tracks was made or where a vehicle was headed at the time may long since have been forgotten, but each machine leaves its brand mingled with a thousand others. In the warm months, as the tracks are worn deeper and flood, the operator moves to one side or the other and cuts a new set of twin scars across the land. In broad fields where work has been extensive, tracks blanket the countryside like the wet rows of a rice paddy; these trails often change the entire drainage pattern. And on slopes they start gullies that can hide a bulldozer. The Alaska Department of Natural Resources now attempts to prohibit cross-country vehicle travel over thawed land. And state law forbids vehicles from crossing or using streams without prior approval of the Alaska Department of Fish and Game.

Along the coast of the Arctic Ocean, oil companies have mined gravel from offshore barrier islands and the shallow lagoons and piled it in long rows waiting to be moved to drill pads and roadways. Waterfowl ecologists point out that these barrier islands provide important protection for myriads of waterfowl during nesting and molting seasons and especially during ice storms. Shallow lagoons, which the islands protect, are feeding areas for thousands of brant. And since the barrier islands influence the salinity of the lagoons by slowing the movement of fresh river water to the sea, some of these areas are important habitat for freshwater fish.

We also saw open dumps, widely scattered oil drums, and drill

Oil drums are a common sight in Arctic Alaska. This pile of drums was produced by the military during World War II.

sites where the operators have finished and moved their rigs but left behind the pilings on which the platforms stood as well as their other cast-off materials. No doubt some of the oil companies realize that they must work hard at their housekeeping in the Arctic. They have their practical reasons. They harbor dreams of moving in on the Arctic Game Range to the east and strive to sugarcoat the destruction they now bring to the North Country.

Handling waste materials from the oil camps is not a simple matter, and as you fly over the oil fields you see varying degrees of efficiency. There are open dumps onto which all refuse from camps, including human wastes, is dumped and left exposed. In summer, slowly rotting garbage creates rich odors to be wafted on the Arctic breezes to the sensitive noses of bears that may be roaming miles inland toward the foothills. Eventually the bears show up at the dumps.

Oil company rules forbid crews in the Arctic to have guns in camp. "But let a bear show up in camp," one state biologist told me, "and there is no shortage of guns to meet the opportunity." The bear that wanders into the oil camp seldom escapes. In the early days of oil work on the North Slope, the crews saw bears frequently. Now they are rare.

Other wildlife, too, is harassed by oil field personnel, especially the helicopter pilots. There have been many reports of helicopters chasing bears and wolves to exhaustion, even in the Arctic National Wildlife Range. You realize, as you spot large animals on the tundra from a plane, how extremely vulnerable they are. They are easy to see, and they have no place to hide. Biologists with both the state and federal governments told me they know definitely that pelts of illegally taken grizzly bears, wolves, and polar bears have been shipped south by company men.

State and federal law enforcement officers are also convinced that rare and endangered birds of prey, including gyrfalcons and peregrines, are being smuggled out of Arctic Alaska for sale to the falconry trade. Some of these raptors have been confiscated at Alaskan airports, but a gyrfalcon can bring $10,000 or considerably more if it reaches the Mideastern countries.

The eyries of gyrfalcons and peregrines are easily spotted from low-flying helicopters, and knowledgeable operators keep maps of their locations.

And at least one well-known bush pilot was moonlighting as a wolf hunter while flying oil company surveys. In the air for long hours, he frequently saw wolves, shot them from the plane, landed, and skinned them. Even after bounty payments for Arctic wolves were stopped, the furs were still worth $100 or more when flown south.

But with the oil, as it comes from the earth, comes the greatest problem and the greatest threat of all — moving the black gold out of the North.

Distance, severe climate, and lack of developed transportation facilities loomed as staggering challenges to the budding North Slope oil industry. There simply is no safe way to ship the great quantity of oil that will come from the Arctic. But the oil industry is accustomed to moving oil, sometimes by fantastic schemes. And the knowledge that it is frequently spilled in the process worries them little as long as public opinion doesn't create too severe a backlash. Transportation of oil out of the Arctic, then, called for the biggest and most costly system ever devised. At least four possible routes were immediately apparent. Oil might be shipped out by extending a rail line to Prudhoe Bay, by transporting it by ship through the Northwest Passage, by pumping it through a giant pipeline southward to an all-weather port in southern Alaska, or by linking up with a pipeline route through central Canada.

Less than a year after the oil strike on the North Slope, Atlantic Richfield, Humble Oil, and British Petroleum Corporation announced that they had become the major partners in a spectacular plan to build a giant oil pipeline southward to Valdez on Prince William Sound. For 800 miles the Trans Alaska Pipeline System, since renamed Alyeska Pipeline Service Company, would lay a steel artery 48 inches in diameter. This pipe would hold 413,285 gallons of oil per mile, and the oil would travel through the pipe at temperatures of about 170 degrees.

Suddenly the specter of a cylinder of hot oil coursing across the tundra brought a flood of questions from engineers and ecologists

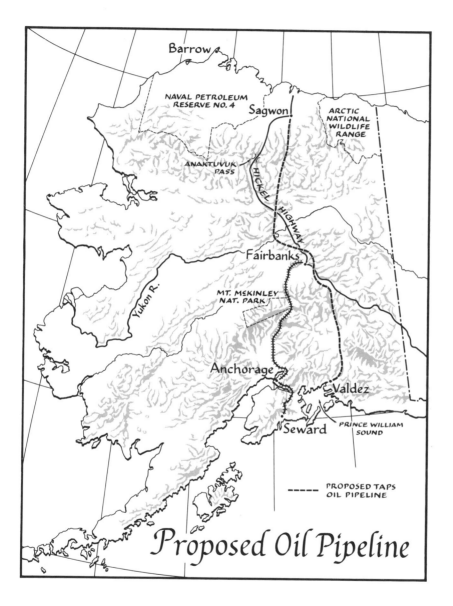

Barrow

NAVAL PETROLEUM
RESERVE NO. 4

Sagwon

ARCTIC
NATIONAL
WILDLIFE
RANGE

ANAKTUVUK
PASS

HICKEL HIGHWAY

Fairbanks

Yukon R.

MT. McKINLEY
NAT. PARK

Anchorage

Valdez

Seward

PRINCE WILLIAM
SOUND

----- PROPOSED TAPS
OIL PIPELINE

Proposed Oil Pipeline

Meanwhile, legal preparations were underway to stop the granting of permits. The native people of Stevens Village on the Yukon obtained, on April 1, an injunction prohibiting construction of either the road or pipeline over a section of the route in the vicinity of the village.

Also at work were attorneys for the Wilderness Society, Friends of the Earth, and the Environmental Defense Fund. The three conservation organizations had joined forces to block Secretary Hickel's plan to grant the pipeline permits. On April 13, they obtained a federal court injunction against building the haul road that would accompany the pipeline over the 390-mile route from the Yukon to Prudhoe Bay, and against granting permits to mine the essential gravel from public lands for the road's construction. The 200-foot-wide right of way which TAPS had asked for its road, and the 100-foot-wide strip requested for the pipeline, allegedly would violate provisions of the 1920 federal Mineral Leasing Act which established a limit of 54 feet on pipeline widths over federal lands.

Also surfacing about this time was strong testimony against the pipeline concept from within the Department of the Interior. The director of the U.S. Geological Survey, Dr. William T. Pecora, stated officially in January that "to bury a hot pipeline in permafrost ground composed of unconsolidated sediments with relatively high ice content could give us grave concern, not because of the melting by itself, but because of the consequences of the melting if safeguards were not designed into the engineering system." Dr. Pecora was also heading a study group surveying the TAPS proposal, and during the spring of 1970 this group's report further questioned the soundness and thoroughness of the advance planning for the pipeline. Dr. Pecora's committee considered it quite possible, in view of the failure of TAPS to show that it had designed a safe plan for installing a hot-oil pipe in permafrost, that both the design and the routing for the project would have to be changed. This testimony was an important factor in the decision of Federal Judge George L. Hart, Jr., who ordered that permits be held up.

The resulting injunctions led Alaska's Governor Keith H. Miller, nervous and impatient because the oil boom seemed to be bogging down, to decide that the federal government was being extremely sticky about the whole issue. He announced that existing law authorized him to issue permits for the project to proceed across federal land, and that he would issue such an order. Few seemed to agree with him. And even with Governor Miller's approval, the oil companies were not much interested in forging ahead in defiance of a federal court order. Appeals and trials could prolong the whole issue for several years and, in theory at least, give the scientific community time to understand better the nature of the Arctic ecosystems that are in jeopardy.

Conservationists around the nation had been asking their representatives to keep a watchful eye on developments on the North Slope, and to see to it that the federal land there was protected from irreversible abuse. On April 8, 1970, the Subcommittee on Conservation and Natural Resources of the House Committee on Government Operations wrote a detailed letter to Secretary Hickel. In substance the letter asked the secretary not to issue the TAPS permit, at least until his department had answered a long list of pertinent questions. All seven members of the subcommittee signed the letter. "There is too much at stake from an environmental standpoint," said the congressmen, "to warrant hasty action." Obviously, Congress had serious doubts that the Department of the Interior had fully studied the potential of the pipeline for damaging the Arctic ecosystem.

But the tundra already carried widespread scars of the initial rush to open trails to the new oil fields. I flew one day down the Yukon River to the "Walter J. Hickel Highway," then northward along this route. The road was first used during the winter of 1968–69. It was also used briefly the following winter. Some expect that it may already have lived out its usefulness, and Governor Miller did not request funds to open it again in the winter of 1970–71.

Alaska conservationists believe this road might better have been designed as a true ice road, with a solid trail of packed ice and snow to support the freight vehicles as they plow northward through the 24-hour-a-day darkness toward Prudhoe Bay. Ice roads can support traffic for a few weeks even after the spring thaw begins. But the Hickel Highway was made at a public expense of $750,000 — for the benefit of the trucking industry — by driving bulldozers through subarctic woodlands and across open tundra to the North Slope, scalping the land to smooth it. Consequently, its ugly dark trench is etched permanently into the landscape, no matter when the road is abandoned.

During the spring thaw the Hickel Highway turns into a quagmire. Some call it "Hickel's canal." Beneath us stretched a chain of puddles and pools where the route crossed low country, making questionable the speculation that this will eventually become a year-round road to the North. "I'd like to canoe the Hickel Highway," one Alaska conservationist told me, "because the portages are so short."

But this is only one of the scars the oil rush has cut into the public lands north of the Yukon. We turned eventually from the Hickel Highway to find the path the pipeline is to follow. How would we find or follow a pipeline not yet built? This proved to be no problem at all. What most people south of the Yukon don't realize is that the oil industry did not wait for the necessary pipeline permits before going to work.

Out of the boreal forest, from the Yukon to Prudhoe Bay, the routes for both the pipeline and the haul road that would service it have already been "prospected" with bulldozers across the gray-green tundra. The trails, along which crews had conducted soil tests, stretched northward ahead of us, sometimes running close together, in other places a mile or more apart where the road and pipeline called for negotiating different types of terrain.

In an open place ahead, a settlement appeared where no native village was marked on the map. As we drew nearer we made out the shape of a large modern construction camp, sitting idle, a man-made island in the wilderness. This was one of five complete construction camps already installed along the TAPS route, and authorized by the Bureau of Land Management. Their total estimated cost was $20 million. One typical camp had 50 trailer units set in rows, the established method of housing Arctic construction crews. There were also long rows of idle trucks and other heavy machinery, as well as giant fuel storage tanks. Each camp had a smooth new landing strip. If oil should eventually be taken from the Arctic Slope by some method other than the TAPS route, the equipment will have to be hauled back out of the North at great financial loss — or left to rot like so much of the military equipment left behind to mar the world's faraway places.

But no one can backhaul his tracks out of the tundra. The scars hastily inflicted on the wild country will be left as stark evidence of the oil companies' arrogant self-confidence in their own power.

In Washington, meanwhile, Secretary of Interior Hickel must have noted that his longtime popularity with the oil community was

With spring thaw, the
"ice road" to the oil fields
becomes a quagmire.
George Laycock

showing weaknesses. The *Arctic Oil Journal,* published in Fairbanks, speculated openly that the reason for the secretary's "turnabout" must lie in his ambition toward higher office. Why else, they wondered, would he "jump on the conservationist bandwagon"?

Gloom blanketed the Alaskan oil community and the political scene in May when Judge Hart further ruled that his temporary injunction be extended and that the Department of the Interior must hold off issuing building permits to TAPS until there has been a full study of the potential ecological damage. Such a study may take several years.

This was exactly what ecologists had been urging all along. The rush for North Slope oil had proceeded at breakneck speed from the day of the Prudhoe Bay announcement. There was not possibly time enough for serious, detailed scientific studies of the tundra ecology, with its unique energy cycles and unusual environmental factors. The oil industry had either ignored this or believed that it might not really matter anyhow. True, they had sent their own parties into the tundra to make inventories and studies of the eco- systems, but there was no reason to believe the oil company scientists could understand the intricate life patterns of the North Slope within a few months, when ecologists not connected with oil believed such studies would require years. The court order would provide the time ecologists had pleaded for.

Meanwhile, the Humble Oil Company's S.S. *Manhattan,* with its 115,000-ton deadweight capacity, made the historic maiden voyage through the Northwest Passage late in the summer of 1969. The big tanker got off to a late start because of the time needed to con- vert it and strengthen it for use as an icebreaker. It was sliced into four sections, which were worked on individually in different ports, then barged back to Philadelphia and rejoined. During its 4500-mile, six-week voyage, the *Manhattan* attracted worldwide attention.

There was little said, however, about the fact that the hull of the *Manhattan* had been ruptured by the ice on her first trip. Without question, if oil is shipped over this north sea route, there will be tankers spreading their cargoes on the frigid waters. And ecologists fear that oil, with its slow rate of natural decomposition, will engulf the world of the polar bear, seal, waterfowl, and fish in a gummy black mess that cannot be cleaned up within our lifetime. Such a possibility has not been lost on the Canadian government, which has since announced that Canada's international boundary extends twelve miles at sea instead of three, and that all of the waters around the Arctic islands lie within Canada.

Prime Minister Pierre Elliott Trudeau told a reporter for the *Christian Science Monitor* that Canada's concern was keeping the Arctic Ocean clean. "We don't want it turned into a cesspool covered with oil," he said. Oil tankers pollute the oceans' waters much more often than is generally known. We hear of the dramatic incidents, the *Torry Canyon*s. But in Alaska's Cook Inlet scarcely a month passes without two or three new oil spills coating the waters and the wildlife. There is no reason to believe the situation would be anything but worse in the Arctic Ocean, with its massive ice packs. Loading facilities for such tankers would likely be built in deep water 30 miles at sea and the oil piped out to these docks.

"Oil companies," says Charles E. Spahr, president of Standard Oil of Ohio, which owns a $27\frac{1}{2}$ percent interest in the Trans Alaska Pipeline System (now the Alyeska Pipeline Service Company), "have been building pipelines for a long time. They are the safest and fastest mode of transporting crude oil." Biologists with whom I talked in Alaska, many of whom have seen numerous oil spills from ships, agree with Spahr's conclusion that a pipeline, despite its own dangers, will be the safest way to move oil out of the Arctic. Even so, there will be spills.

The question then becomes one of where the pipeline will run, and here there are more possibilities than the Alyeska suggestion. One alternate route would run eastward to the Canadian Arctic. Recent oil discoveries in northern Canada have prompted Canadians to move ahead with plans for a pipeline south to Edmonton, Alberta, from which oil can be shipped to any part of North America.

Alaskan oil from the Prudhoe Bay area could be piped to the Mackenzie Delta. From there the big pipeline could, it is said, carry the crude all the way up the Mackenzie River, a route that would keep it off the delicate tundra.

But between the Mackenzie Delta and the Alaska oil fields lies the Arctic National Wildlife Range — which deserves strict wilderness protection. The shallow offshore waters are state lands, and one suggestion is to place the pipe beyond the low-lying barrier islands and the lagoons where the brant feed.

No matter how the oil comes out of the Arctic it will spill and drip and inflict its smothering damage on living ecosystems. Prince William Sound, if the oil docks are built and the tankers loaded there, will bear its sheen of oil repeatedly, just as Cook Inlet does now. In the Arctic even the drippings from abandoned "empty" drums can pollute waterfowl habitat. And the more relaxed the controls over the oil industry, the greater the damage will become.

Throughout much of Alaska there is deep resentment against outsiders urging a more thoughtful approach to exploiting the North Slope oil. "If you want to make a whole state into a national park," one Alaskan said, "why don't you turn Ohio into a national park?"

"All of that north country," another Alaskan told me, "used to be 'our Arctic wasteland.' Now suddenly it becomes 'our precious tundra.'" And one of Alaska's state senators recently proclaimed that he was sick of "carpetbaggers" coming in and telling Alaskans how to manage their affairs.

But Alaska has its own dedicated conservationists, among them some of the most knowledgeable and able scientists anywhere. "The resources they're talking about," one of these men said to me, "belong to all of us. What some of these people want to do has been done forty-eight times before. Where's the big rush? You would think there is time to plan man's activities in this state, time to do it right."

Time, however, is what the Alaska business community, as well as the oil company manipulators from outside, will not permit themselves. When things do not go their way, the business interests have a handy scapegoat in the conservation movement. Shortly after the court order that stopped the oil pipeline and haul road, I spoke with an official of one of the major airlines working in Alaska. "There has already been too much written and said about the North Slope," he told me. "We know that. That's why the pipeline has stopped. These people against it are responsible for serious hardship in Alaska now. The town of Valdez is going broke," he added. "And one airline is likely to go bankrupt there this year." When you check deeper into these charges, you find that the airline in question over-extended itself as the result of the oil industry's high-speed rush on the North Slope and that it was already in deep trouble before Judge Hart's court order. Or you find that the oil industry arrogantly forged ahead, spending huge sums, firmly convinced that no one could stop it.

Without question, North Slope oil will be profitable enough to accommodate the cost of whatever measures are needed to protect the environment, both in the oil fields and along transportation

One of the many unnamed mountains in the Arctic National Wildlife Range.

routes. Oil companies often speak of the towering costs of operating under Arctic conditions. But they also realize that they stand to reap enormous returns on their investments. Economist Dr. Arlon R. Tussing, of the Federal Field Committee for Development Planning in Alaska, told a Department of the Interior hearing on the pipeline project: "Under present tax rates, the anticipated rate of return to these companies [Atlantic Richfield, Humble, and British Petroleum] together on exploration, development, and production would be about forty-three percent." Even if the cost of the pipeline were to double, the companies could, according to Dr. Tussing's calculations, still anticipate returns of about 36 percent.

Thorough programs of environmental protection should be standard parts of the cost of production. Backhauling trash from the oil fields should be the unquestioned procedure for all of the operators, and the oil companies should also pay the costs of government inspectors to police their operations.

But what can housekeeping do to save this delicately balanced Arctic ecosystem? Careful procedures can minimize the damages, but what you realize as you fly over this country is that these North Slope oil fields can be written off as wilderness once the drill rigs and their crews have moved in. This land is no longer what it was even two years ago. And soon pipelines, little and big, will cross and crisscross the land, cutting into patches the open tundra where the caribou roamed. "In the space of a few months," ecologist Dr. Robert B. Weeden of the University of Alaska has said, "oil explorations have destroyed the wilderness character of an area in northern Alaska bigger than the state of Massachusetts."

The oil companies may hire all the ecologists they can find, backhaul every stick of trash to Fairbanks and beyond, and practice the finest housekeeping they know. They may deal firmly with their subcontractors, as they must, and cooperate fully with state inspectors. But the fact remains that they will scar this land irreparably. In short, these lands which have been turned over to oil are, in no sense, multiple-use acres. This is oil country, and a brief two years of oil work proved that the scars can be neither erased nor repaired.

Elsewhere, time is short on Alaska's North Slope. The Arctic National Wildlife Range is our last chance to preserve any of the American Arctic as it was when we inherited the continent. What has happened along the North Slope makes it imperative that we move rapidly to protect this refuge from the ravages of the oil people. Pitted against the conservationists in their desires to preserve this wild northeast corner of Alaska is a bold industry — big, rich, and muscular.

And there is no question that the oilmen are looking covetously toward the Arctic National Wildlife Range. "We are almost certain to see pressure build up," says Dr. Weeden, "to allow seismic exploration and oil or mineral leasing on the range."

Time is short. Unless the Arctic National Wildlife Range is given solid protection within the next years, the chances that it will follow the Prudhoe Bay area on the sacrificial altar of the oil industry are excellent.

The answer lies in the promise of nailing down securely an official wilderness designation of this entire refuge. From the air, the contrast between this land and the North Slope oil fields is startling. By comparison, few trails mark the Wildlife Range. Its slopes and valleys lie beneath the cool Arctic sun as they have for centuries. Out in the foothills, thousands of caribou cows spread over a 20- or 30-mile area with the first of spring's new wobbly-legged calves. Half a dozen times we spotted barren ground grizzly bears standing exposed on the open tundra. They would be the first but not the last to go if oil invades their refuge.

Gone also would be the wild character of the land, gone with the exploiters and developers as surely as Prudhoe Bay has. And we would have taken one more irrevocable step, sending Alaska — our last state to be developed — down the same unplanned trail along which we have pushed almost all other lands entrusted to us.

Common loon. *Michael Wotton*

Index

Index